Sweeping Beauty

Sweeping

CONTEMPORARY
WOMEN POETS
DO HOUSEWORK

Beauty

Edited by Pamela Gemin

University of Iowa Press | Iowa City

University of Iowa Press, Iowa City 52242

Copyright © 2005 by the University of Iowa Press

All rights reserved

Printed in the United States of America

Design by April Leidig-Higgins

http://www.uiowa.edu/uiowapress

The University of Iowa Press is a member of Green
Press Initiative and is committed to preserving natural
resources.

Printed on acid-free paper

Library of Congress Cataloging-in-Publication Data
Sweeping beauty: contemporary women poets do
housework / edited by Pamela Gemin.
   p.   cm.
Includes index.
ISBN 0-87745-968-1 (pbk.)
1. Housekeeping—Poetry.   2. American poetry—
Women authors.   3. American poetry—20th century.
4. American poetry—21st century.   I. Gemin,
Pamela, 1954–.
PS595.H69S94 2005
811'.540803552—dc22   2005041921

05 06 07 08 09 P 5 4 3 2 1

This book is for my mother,
Patricia O'Connor Pierce,
and for my grandmothers and aunts,
all fine housekeepers.

Contents

Acknowledgments

Thanks to my family — Mom, Dad, and Joe — and to the friends and colleagues who continue to support and sustain in both tidy and messy times, especially Becky, Ellen, Jan, Julie, Paula, P. K., Rich and Sue, and Ron. I am grateful as well to Kristi, Laurie, and Ryan for their help with typing and proofing, and to the Faculty Development Program at the University of Wisconsin Oshkosh for the grant support that made this project possible. And once again, I thank Holly Carver and everyone at the University of Iowa Press for their wonderful, important work.

Introduction

Stay Where I Can See You

In memories of early childhood, the preschool days spent at home with my mother in our yellow house along the railroad tracks, there is always the length of white rubber-coated clothesline stretched in triplicate between two wooden posts cemented into our backyard lawn. There the business of our everyday lives was spread out to wave in the crisp light of day: my father's white cotton shirts fresh from the ringer, my mother's floral print housedresses and solid blue aprons edged with eyelet. My father's striped cotton pajamas and my mother's pink nylon shorties hung on the line with my own fuzzy footed pajamas and ribbed T-shirts, my miniature blue jeans with their plaid flannel cuffs. Every two weeks my Red Ball Jets bobbed, hanging by their tongues in the hinges of clothespins my mother saved for heavier wash, alongside my stuffed rabbit, Easter, pinned to the line by his raggedy ears. Sheets and towels rippled strategically on the outside lines as our underwear quivered inside, safe from the neighbors' view. There, under the inside line, below briefs and brassieres, flanked by sugar-and-lemon sheets and pillowcases, I skipped a length of heaven inside the billowing pastel walls, inhaling the "magic outdoor freshness" of my mother's daytime world.

If she was discontent in her career as an ex–beauty operator and full-time housewife, my mother never dropped a hint in my direction. Sure, she let go her share of sighs. But now, when I think of what laundry day really meant for her before and after the clean wash was hung, I realize that her excursions from the little laundry room off our kitchen to the backyard line, hauling basket after basket of our wadded wet clothes on her hip, might well have been the sweetest part of the job — an outdoor respite between the gathering, sorting, collar-scrubbing, bleach-soaking, and wringing that preceded and the sprinkling, steam ironing, folding, and sorting that followed. And even as our clean clothes waved in the backyard breeze like flags announcing to the neighborhood and to the United States of America that my mother was doing her job, somewhere another piece of our clothing, stained with workday ink or sweat or slopped with chicken grease or ketchup, readied itself for her big wicker hamper.

"Stay where I can see you," my mother would warn as she went back inside to peel the potatoes and season the roast she would slow-cook for supper until it almost fell apart. "I want to be able to see you out the kitchen window, okay? When you can't see the stripes on the curtains, come back toward the house till you can. Got it?" If I stayed where my mother could see me, within the invisible fencing of her field of vision, I could run up and down the lines of drying clothes to the edge of our yard, where the railroad property began. She could see me stopping to pick the snapdragons and daisies that studded that unmown border or weaving fairy shawls from its tall sticks of brittle grass. But what else did my mother see as she scraped and washed and rinsed and dried and stacked the dishes, scoured the sink, dried and washed and dried her hands again? Was she making a list in her head? Worrying, praying, daydreaming? Did she sing?

If she had written them, what would my mother's poems be about? This was the question foremost in my thoughts as I began to collect the pieces for this anthology. Would she write about the world outside the kitchen window, blooming and freezing and melting down again? The train whistle roaring outside the bedroom she shared with my father, thin blankets passed down sister to sister? Her trips to the market, snot-nosed daughter riding along in the cart and whining for some expensive brand of cereal? Juice-stained fingernails, snakes in the berry rows, pot lids rattling on the burner? Mason jars scalding, canning seals popping, the sweet, seedy taste of jam? Mothers like mine, from the World War II generation, inhabit many of the poems in this book, as do the ancestral women of family trees and fables. Marilyn Chin celebrates a village elder in "The Floral Apron," and Kimberly Blaeser praises the female ancestors by listing the miracles they worked by lamplight. The kitchen, still heart and center of the home, is the setting for a significant number of poems, including one in which Joy Harjo speculates that it might also be the place the world began and the place it will end. In Dorothy Barresi's "In Waking Words," a fifties mother, her refrigerator "so turquoise it hurts," dozes at the kitchen table, "a commuter except / she is already at home, at work." Across town, the mother in Holly Iglesias's prose poem series, "Feeding Frenzy," "twirl[s] around the kitchen in Capri pants and ballerina flats, a Camel smoking on the windowsill above appliances."

In her oral history of 1950s women, Brett Harvey includes a chapter titled "Post Doc or Paella?" in which she refers to a college president's call for courses in clothing and textiles, house-planning and interior decoration as well as "the theory and presentation of a Basque Paella, a well-marinated shish-ke-bab, [and] lamb kidneys sautéed in sherry." She also provides a few words from Adlai Stevenson's 1955 graduation address to the women of Smith College, who, while they could not directly contribute to his vision of a free-thinking society could, in "the humble role of housewife," influence their clueless husbands. (Sylvia Plath was in that audience, and I have always wondered whether she was taking note of Stevenson's message or daydreaming a poem.)

Baby boom daughters, too, were raised to be housekeepers but advised to educate themselves toward a career "as something to fall back on." The young college women I teach today don't believe me when I quote that phrase or share the old joke that women went to college for "M-R-S." degrees. The message was clear: you will always be cooking, sewing, washing, scrubbing, and dusting, but you might also have to do a stint as a *career girl* before you get married. Or if your husband dies or ditches you or, God forbid, if you don't ever catch a man . . . so you'd better learn to type. Little did our guidance counselors know what was in store for us girls raised in the fifties and sixties, for whom housewifery would soon come to be known as a sucker's profession despite limited opportunities for careers outside the home and the inevitable thud of the glass ceiling.

My home economics teacher, a stout and bespectacled model of patience, stifled her sighs as she tried to untangle the masses of thread sewn into the base of my zippers. She taught us to make white sauce and prune whip, two foods whose names alone frightened and depressed me. My white sauce was lumpy and yellow, my prune whip a flat paste fit for no man. I cheated in typing class; by coughing loudly before the starting bell I could clatter in the date and the "Dear Sir" address before the honest girls began. These were the days of the secretarial typing pools, those cavernous rooms full of women we saw in the background in big-city movies, slapping their carriages back in alert synch, hoping to catch the eye of the handsome, Rock Hudson-y boss, who tripped in after a three-martini lunch.

Meanwhile, at home, we had weekly lists of chores. One of the first I learned was to sweep the porch and sidewalk with the tall corn broom my mother called the *good* broom, not to be confused with the ratty old nylon-bristled broom she used to sweep the garage and basement or the whisk broom she could whip from its nail in the closet to catch the caked clots of spring mud the moment they dropped from our boot soles onto her kitchen linoleum. Sweeping, she inferred, was an art: there was one true, original way to sweep and many ways not to. You didn't flop your arms in loose strokes; you kept them tight into your hips. You didn't waste time sweeping in one direction; you kept momentum by sweeping side to side, stepping along briskly as you worked. You didn't dawdle. The dirt was not going anywhere unless you took it away on the current of your broom. You concentrated on your job until its original purpose fell away and only its scrape-whoosh rhythm remained.

My mother could have written a book about sweeping. Whether she loved or hated the job, she took it seriously, as her grandmother had, as her mother and sisters did. She wrote "sweep the porch and sidewalk" first on my list of chores to be checked off as I completed them. But sweeping, like hanging wash or polishing furniture, could also be hypnotic. If the sweeper let herself go, leaned into the task, nudged the dust from sidewalk cracks and porch slats, from the corners of her own head, who knew what she might stir up? And what if she dared to put down her broom, pick up a pen, and follow the wide-open paths of her daydreams in the privacy of her own home? For many, housekeeping provides the key to the temporary realm of what Mihaly Csikszentmihalyi calls "flow," a state of mind approaching meditation, in which one's absorption in a task obliterates time, space, and circumstance, a state of mind also conducive to making poetry.

Gone in the Motion

"Some people ask me why I wrote a series of poems about housekeeping if I'm a feminist," Julia Alvarez says in an essay on formal poetry included in Annie Finch's A Formal Feeling Comes, and rather than seeing the housekeeper's role as limiting Alvarez states simply: "These were the crafts we women had, sewing, embroidering, spinning, sweeping, even the lowly dusting. And as Dylan Thomas said, 'we sang in our chains like the sea.'" In "How I Learned to Sweep," Alvarez's young speaker has been handed a broom and told to sweep until her mother's floor is "immaculate." When her task is complete, she turns on the television to see helicopters crashing into the jungle in Vietnam and picks up her broom again, metaphorically sweeping away their wreckage.

Alvarez says that she wrote the poem in rhymed couplets to mirror the dance shared by broom and sweeper. "My idea of traditional forms is that as women much of our heritage is trapped in them. But the cage can turn into a house if you housekeep it the right way," she claims. "You housekeep it by working the words just so."

If we accept Alvarez's premise that "the cage can turn into a house," we might accept Gaston Bachelard's notion, set forth in his Poetics of Space, that "the house protects the dreamer," shelters her in her practice of daydreaming. According to Bachelard, the housekeeper's "daydreams . . . keep vigilant watch over the house [and] link its immediate past to its immediate future." He explains how housework can be "transformed into a creative activity": "The minute we apply a glimmer of consciousness to a mechanical gesture . . . we sense new impressions . . . beneath this familiar domestic duty. For consciousness rejuvenates everything, giving a quality of beginning to the most everyday actions . . . and so when a poet rubs a piece of furniture . . . he creates a new object. . . . [H]e registers this object officially as a member of the human household."

Consider Deborah Digges's marvelous poem "Broom," ode to a "broom whose stave is pine or hickory, / and whose skirt [is] of birch-spray and heather." Not until halfway through the poem does the speaker even mention the broom, but this object is invested with more and more meaning as the poem gathers speed. Images of the speaker's house — its unlocked doors, its sinks, and its beds "above which . . . threefold dreams collided" — are tender ones, seemingly lit from inside. But more than anything else, the speaker tells us, she has loved a broom, which she describes as rustic, its bristles "parted one way like [her] hair." In the course of her poem, Digges's sweeper personifies her broom, but it seems she doesn't so much love the object itself as the image of herself sweeping. And her declaration of broom-love turns the poem and gets to the question at its heart: "Once I asked myself, when was I happy?"

As a reader, I wanted very much to know the answer to that question, as well as the next: "When did the light hold me and I didn't struggle?" The speaker's struggling to escape the light is most revealing; she is asking *when did I trust my happiness enough not to fight it?* And those images of her sweeping the threshold of each season's debris come to her in reply, and those of her dancing with the broom, and even those of her breaking out windows with it "as if the house were burning" with the recognition of her man's unfaithfulness: "And so the broom became / an oar that parted waters . . . or twirled / around and around on the back lawn, / a sort of compass through whose blurred counter-motion / the woods became a gathering of brooms, / onlooking and ancestral," as in a fairy tale. In fact, there's a lot of the domestic fairy tale in this poem's themes of enchantment and transformation, also present in Heid Erdrich's "Sweeping Heaven," a poem in which the sweeper abandons her job of sweeping God's throne and hurls herself down through space, "a blue-white, gem-hard point" that cuts a hole in the sky. According to Bachelard, "housewifely care weaves the ties that unite a very ancient past to the new epoch. The housewife awakens [what] has been asleep." In the end, Erdrich's broom goddess enters through "a girl's unblinking eye, and settle[s] below her throat. / . . . until she feels swept through inside / by something restless . . . opening so wide / it showers like the wheeling prairie sky." Digges's speaker, too, takes on her broom's movements, sweeping her hair first across her sons' backs and then across her lover's body, "lost swaying" and "gone in the motion." In this way, she, like Erdrich's sweeper, reinvents the act of sweeping.

In his chapter "House and Universe," Bachelard includes a passage by Henri Bosco, in which Bosco describes his housekeeper's "revery into work, of [vast] dreams into the humblest of occupations": "When she washed a sheet or . . . polished a brass candlestick, little movements of joy mounted from the depths of her heart, enlivening her household tasks." The housekeeper, Bosco claimed, would "contemplate to her heart's content the supernatural images" that arose in the flow of her work, as if "she washed, dusted, and swept in the company of angels."

He adds a passage from the poet Rilke who, when his maid was away, set to the task of polishing his own furniture, donning her "big apron and little washable suede gloves": "I was . . . magnificently alone . . . under my zealous dustcloth [the piano] started to purr mechanically . . . and its fine, deep black surface became more and more beautiful. When you've been through this there's little you don't know!"

Rilke also senses "the friendliness" of the objects he cleaned, senses that they are "happy to be so well treated," and confesses that in housekeeping he "felt moved, as though something were happening . . . which was not purely superficial but immense, and which touched my very soul." He imagines then that he is "the emperor washing the feet of the poor."

Did my mother, down on her hands and knees with a scrub brush and a pail of cooling water full of gritty Spic and Span, ever imagine she was an empress? I am certain she did not. I doubt if she even compared herself to Cinderella, the household princess whose years of quiet drudgery paid off in royal riches (though Denise Duhamel has a different fate in store for Cindy here, in "The Ugly Step Sister"). But she must have drifted, as I do now, into and out of her housework, "gone in the motion" of the brush and the wave of the rinsing rag. If the sparkling stove and refrigerator smiled their appreciation, they did so only in television commercials. But my mother had the satisfaction, however momentary, that she was doing her job, that her job mattered, that her family needed a clean floor: the dirt had been there and now it was gone. Even though she was a Catholic girl raised with the stories of the saints, I doubt that housework made my mother feel holy, though it may have martyred her now and then or transformed her the way it transformed her house. And if ever she was "in the company of angels" when she polished and scrubbed, they flew the coop as soon as we devils came rolling home with our muddy shoes. But Rilke may be on to something when he hints that housekeepers can tend to their inner lives while they tend to their houses.

In an essay entitled "The Care-Givers," poet Maxine Kumin explores the ways in which her writing process and practice have changed since the early fifties, when she began her vocation. Back then, she says, "the stewpot of discontent in which I simmered had no name, no authenticity, no support group." Kumin told herself that she would sell a poem by the time her third child was born, and with the sale of her first poem to the *Christian Science Monitor*, she was able to "carry on this business without in any way neglecting housewifery and motherhood. . . . The Muse had to stumble along subsisting on crumbs of time." When she eventually established her writing routine, Kumin says, she "found [herself] drawing heavily on domestic experience," adding that "many of [her] first poems came up out of dailiness to form what [she has] since come to call 'tribal' poems — poems of family, of connectedness, of blood relationships and bonding."

And readers, I think, still expect women to write our tribal poems. As I continue to note, happily, that more and more male poets are encroaching upon the domestic turf — sometimes as if no one else had ever made a pot of soup or crushed a clove of garlic before — I can't help it: I prefer to read tribal poems in the voices of women. They are instantly accessible, authentic, and sincere by default. And while Kumin refers to a quote by writer Margaret Walker, who offers that women writers' "critical decisions . . . are questions of compromise, and of guilt," Kumin answers, "I like to think a little guilt makes the world go round and that the ability to compromise deserves high marks, for it is a learned skill. The life inside my poems was worth whatever it took to get there: guilt and compromise, tenacity, an inner secrecy that hid behind the facade of suburban housewife." Speaking of the women writers Kumin says she most admires, she says she is "drawn to them by way of affirmation, a sharing of insights. . . . Ideally, caring is genderless. . . . In the real world, however, we are still the primary care-givers, and this is the world we live in and must write about."

In Gailmarie Pahmeier's "Sunday Baking," included in this anthology, a housewife in the act of kneading bread is observed unawares by her husband, who is outside on their porch, "smoking and reading an easy magazine" as she works: "The bread's in the oven, and the smell / of love is thick inside, and he knows / that the bread, the woman, and the house are not his, / that this is what is meant by home."

What is the breadmaker thinking about, and why is she smiling? She will take pleasure in sharing her bread, but what the woman dreams into the motion of her kneading is private, and the house is *her* domain. In Pahmeier's poem we see an indication of the "inner secrecy" that Kumin refers to, the tension between women's outside expectations and inside longing or resentment, between orderly satin surfaces and crazy quilts of flip-side texture. And few writers can convey that tension as well as writer Laura Kasischke.

Kasischke's House

Laura Kasischke's work mines the inner territory of the housewife by blasting a series of peepholes into the images that surround her. No woman I have known who has read Kasischke has failed to become instantly inhabited by her voice and vision. Born in 1961, she is the author of seven volumes of poetry (including *Housekeeping in a Dream*, which I gratefully acknowledge as the cornerstone of this anthology) and three novels. Kasischke's work, says Marge Piercy, is "an extraordinary vision of the lives of ordinary women," a description supported by the *Michigan Quarterly Review*, which calls hers "a poetry of the entangled passionate and familial tragedies that poets in postwar America have opted to write into the public record." Likewise, says James Harms, "Kasischke peels back the blander surfaces . . . as if to find the unconscious realm just behind the Formica." And this is what I admire most about her work, Kasischke's relentless probe into the inner lives and imaginations of her female characters, many of whom are housewives on the verge of charring breakfast, smashing dishes, or shooting up the Piggly Wiggly. While only three of Laura Kasischke's poems ("Dinner," "Housekeeping in a Dream," and "The Visibility of Spirits") are included in this anthology, I will refer to some of her other work as it relates to the housekeeper's traditional role.

In "To Whom It May Concern," from Kasischke's *Wild Brides*, the speaker is advertising herself for marriage ("Please please marry me") with this résumé: "I stayed indoors / and rattled the cups brained / the tomatoes . . . until / the teapot shrieked / . . . and the shoe tree bloomed in the closet." The speaker describes the "toaster's terrible grin" and begs to be released from the house. The poem is eerily reminiscent of Sylvia Plath's "The Applicant," in which a potential husband is told about the virtues of a potential wife who is "willing . . . / To bring teacups and roll away headaches / And do whatever you tell it." It's the kind of writing Kasischke does best, tilting and rearranging familiar domestic images — toasters, teapots, and shoe trees — inside a sinister landscape.

The title poem of *Housekeeping in a Dream* (included in this anthology) begins at the kitchen sink: "The sky is a piece of mind / outside the kitchen window, the dishes / the dirt." Outside the window looms the land beyond the fence line, and while the dishes ground the speaker in the kitchen, her mother's voice "whispers / how to do it / in my ear *make a list, make / a meal that will last / all week on Sunday, lie / to your husband . . . / . . . vacuum / like it matters.*" This poem, too, relies on the speaker's reflective powers to push home its premise that the sky is a "piece of mind" beyond reach, that as soon as she begins to think beyond her window frame, the dream will deliver her mother's inescapable mantra of advice, her rules for living. "Vacuum like it matters" is a perfect phrase, easy to imagine on a bumper sticker or as a line from an Elvis Costello song. But it's also a serious piece of advice for a housewife: vacuum as if your vacuuming had purpose and place in the grand scheme, as if it could get you a promotion or a raise or a grant anywhere out there beyond your living room. "I open the freezer and stare at the frost," says Kasischke's zombiefied housekeeper, and as if this dream weren't frightening enough, the punch line, "Perhaps / there was a meal / of dusk and love I should have made / but it's too late," is the chilliest part of the poem.

The collection of poems in *Housekeeping in a Dream* is foreshadowed by an opening poem printed entirely in italics and titled only in the table of contents as *"Crows' Feet."* "'They've found where the universe ends, and it ends / in . . . a pan / of dishsoap soaking / in a greasy sky," the speaker announces, calling up with an almost instinctive immediacy—for any woman who's watched her mother look out the kitchen window longingly while doing dishes or practiced the same ritual herself —the feel of greasy, lukewarm, bubble-spotted water slipping between ungloved fingers.

Yet short of befriending Mr. Coffee, there are many ways to incorporate the imagination into domestic chores. Housekeeping can indeed be a creative, fulfilling activity for a woman even if it doesn't make her rich. "Homemaking," as it was called when I was a girl, does not always sweep one away into the numb drudgery of dustpans and frozen dinners. Several poems here, like Jill Breckenridge's "Cooking Catalogue," Sharon Olds's "Bread," and Natasha Sajé's "What I Want to Make for You," celebrate cooking's sensual joys and healing powers. In several more, the tradition of offering home-cooked food is celebrated as part of women's sympathy and solidarity. "I learned to believe I had the power to ease / awful pains . . . / Like a doctor I learned to create / from another's suffering my own usefulness, and once / you know how to do this, you can never refuse." Julia Kasdorf's sentiments, expressed in "What I Learned from My Mother," are echoed here in poems by Kristin Kovacic and Jesse Lee Kercheval, whose speakers lovingly prepare meals for the ill and grieving.

My mother has always loved to cook. My father still talks about his days as a newlywed graduate student, when his buddies would unwrap their stale bologna sandwiches, limp pickles, and store-bought cookies on the library steps and smirk while my father polished off his homemade Cornish pasty with flank steak and rutabaga, still warm in its tinfoil wrapper, and a thick slab of my mother's blueberry pie. Her early rising, her sifting and chopping and pastry blending was, and still is, her way of loving us out loud, and her kitchen, still avocado green, has always been the center of her universe, the place where she shines brightest.

Most days, I too make good meals for my husband and myself, almost always from scratch and almost always balanced with the healthful ingredients—whole grains and pasta, lean meats, fruits and vegetables—and flavorful seasonings recommended by state-of-the-art cookbooks: fresh garlic, homegrown rosemary and basil, extra-virgin olive oil. Our cooking also has built a strong bridge between my mother and me. When I call and ask how long for the pork roast, how many onions in the soup, what kind of apples in the pie, I am learning the secrets of the tribe.

But slogging home from a late meeting with the groceries, then rummaging in the cupboards for a clean pan, I wonder what it might be like to be married to a man who cooks, to come home and smell my dinner cooking, to have it served to me on clean dishes while I watch Peter Jennings, and then to have those dishes whisked away, never having rinsed out the bloody shrink wrap or stripping the fat and fascia off the chicken with the wrong kind of knife.

"My mother tried to teach me how / to put a little food in each man's mouth," says the speaker in Laura Kasischke's "Dinner" (from *Housekeeping in a Dream*, included in this anthology), as she and her husband sit down to a microwaved meal, while outside the house "the foggy dusk / turns nuclear blue / . . . and smogs up under the kitchen door / and through the cracks in the kitchen walls." The meal itself is "a radio-wave that bounces / electromagnetic between" them, and the couple, we are told, has "been out of butter and sugar for years."

Kasischke's warping of the domestic landscape has earned comparisons to Joyce Carol Oates in reviews of both her poetry and fiction. In Kasischke's second novel, *White Bird in a Blizzard*, the narrator's (Katrina's) suburban housewife mother, Eve, scrubs her sink

> with something chemical and harsh, but powdered, something dyed ocean blue to disguise its deadly powers for the housewives . . . who bought it, only dimly realizing that what they had purchased with its snappy name (Spic and Span, Mr. Clean, Fantastik) was pure acid. The blue of a child's eyes, the blue of a robin's egg—But swallow a teaspoon of that and it will turn your intestines to lace.

Katrina continually imagines scenes from her mother's daily life:

> I pictured her scrubbing the toilet, disinfecting.
> I pictured her in the kitchen, baking angry batches of cookies.
> I saw her in the basement, wringing the necks of my father's white shirts while a choir of nasty children sang '*Ring around the collar! Ring around the collar!*' in her head.
> I saw her in the living room running the vacuum over and over a four-inch area of carpet, seeing something in there that the huge rattling suction of her machine could not suck up.

"A woman *is* her mother. / That's the main thing," Anne Sexton reminds us in "Housewife," and in poems like "Double Image," "Little Girl, My String Bean, My Lovely Woman," or "Pain for a Daughter," she elaborates on this claim. Alicia Ostriker calls Sexton's poem "a critique of marriage as well as a definition of conventional womanhood," and both Kat and her mother would agree, I think, that Sexton is right on target: "Some women marry houses / It's another kind of skin; it has a heart, / a mouth, a liver and bowel movements. / The walls are permanent and pink. / See how she sits on her knees all day, / faithfully washing herself down." Sarah Messer's "Some women marry houses," included here, borrows its title from Sexton and uses the same kind of blurring and overlapping in telling the story of three generations of family women through their relationships to houses and domesticity.

White Bird's Eve has indeed married a house, and what Kat learns from Eve's suffering seems to motivate Kat's sexual experimentation, unaware though she is that her mother is doing some experimenting of her own. Kat pretends not to identify with her mother, yet she spends most of the novel obsessively trying to figure her out. Ostriker points to Sexton's "Housewife" as an example of women's "fixed identification with house, body, mother, [and] her domestic and biological genesis and identity."

Kat calls her family's basement "fifteen cubic feet of limbo," at once "the great, white, humming brain of [the] house" and its "personal wasteland." My favorite girlhood trick was to stand on a chair in our basement and push creepy things — a fat caterpillar, a rubber spider, the head of my fake mink stole with its hinged mouth gaping — into the hole in our kitchen floor below the cupboards, for my mother to stumble upon as she innocently reached for a box of saltines or a can of tuna. As ashamed as I felt afterward, it was thrilling to hear my mother scream — she so seldom raised her voice. In fact, I honestly don't remember my mother complaining about housework, at least not to me, whereas in Kasischke's houses women's anger rises not only in its pure, raging form but in furious humor. Kat imagines suburban housewives' passive aggression as they struggle to remain composed and ladylike in the face of their creeping anger: "a suburban housewife imagines herself slapping a bad waitress, or punching a meddlesome librarian in the stomach: She is polite, she'd never do it. Instead she might wad up a piece of gum and stick it under a chair, hoping the librarian would find it there years later and have to scrape it off with a knife."

In Stealing the Language Alicia Ostriker talks about how far the poetry of feminist writers has come in its expression of anger: "The release of what we could call suppressed passion [is] one of the most recognizable signs of the new poetry," she says, and she adds a few pages later that "like charity, women's anger begins at home." Now that we are managing houses of our own, how can we help but wonder what sinister thoughts our mothers may have had as they basted the pot roast?

Kasischke's "Thunder, or A Place in the Sun" (Housekeeping in a Dream) revisits the male gods alluded to in an earlier poem, "Suburbia." The poem's first section sets the scene of another classic Kasischke kitchen: "The gods are bowling / in heaven tonight. Their wives / cry into / their own black hair / while the kitchen's strange machinery minces / and hatches. / I arrange this. / I arrange that. / I move from room to room."

Short lines and wide expanses in the last three stanzas help to establish the housewife's sluggish tedium, her simmering anger as she stumbles around in the house clueless as to how her feelings should be, as the pop psychologists say, "managed." Kasischke's images seem to have been sprayed with Betty Friedan's "feminine mystique," the strange condition housewives reported to their doctors in the early days of feminism's second wave. Likewise, in "Godmother's Advice" (from *Wild Brides*), a younger woman gets a foreshadowing glimpse of an older women's discontent, untempered by hope or even longing. "Remember: the world is vulgar and everything in it: / the sweet of the melon / and the meat pie steam of being alive. / You will be crying / for more of that."

A Good Tired

Though my mother has dedicated her life to the service of her family, she scarcely fits the June Cleaver housewife mold. But all these years later, Virginia Woolf's angel in the house, the self-denying caregiver content with the least appealing cut of meat, the loaf's heel, and the most uncomfortable chair, still dies hard, especially when it comes to housework. Heid Erdrich describes her as the "Good Woman" whose "house or trailer or apartment / smells of the crockpot simmering bone and broth" and who "goes on waiting in the cold / for visitation, vision, benediction."

"What good does it do anyone," asks Dorianne Laux in "The Idea of Housework," a poem she wrote especially for this anthology, "to have a drawer full of clean knives / . . . your face / reflected eight times over / in the oval bowls of spoons?" But sooner or later, *somebody* has to do the housework. And then there are those days, however rare, when doing housework actually feels good—those laundry Saturdays in late spring, for instance, when a woman might prefer to hang a load of wash outdoors rather than cram it into the dryer. Perhaps it's too easy to romanticize laundry, but there's nothing sweeter smelling than the first line-dried sheets of the season and nothing much lovelier than slipping between them the first night of open screens. Maybe it's the fact that we no longer have to hang our clothes outdoors to dry that makes it romantic to do so, like baking our own bread or sewing our own curtains. In this collection, housework is romanticized as often as it is shunned or satirized, and I imagine that one could write a celebratory housework poem in the morning and a sarcastic housework poem in the evening, any given day of the week. Laux concludes her poem with lines of praise: "Oh to rub the windows with vinegar . . . / . . . Oh the bleachy, / waxy, soapy perfume of spring." There are poems here that sing of housework's saving graces, the gone-in-the-motion comfort and healing found in simple, repetitive moves of making. In "After the Miscarriage," Diane

Gilliam Fisher's speaker deals with her grief in the act of knitting: "It makes sense to my arm, what I am doing . . . maybe it will save me."

"I'm tired," my Grandma O'Connor would say after baking half a dozen of her famous French Canadian pork pies or sugaring a batch of her doughnuts, "but it's a *good* tired." As her own mother was, as her five daughters were, and as many of her granddaughters would be, my grandmother was a housewife. Before that she was a country schoolteacher, and before that a servant who ate, separately from the family she worked for, bowls of plain noodles or rice and ironed their children's ruffled petticoats with an enormous heavy iron she heated in the fireplace. As the story goes, a group of women came to her employers' door one day and removed my grandmother from the house, explaining that she had been mistreated long enough and that they had found her a more suitable housekeeping position. A French Canadian immigrant born in Quebec, she found in her marriage to my grandfather the assurance that she would be provided for. In return my grandfather got to live in the tidiest, cleanest house in northern Wisconsin, if not the entire upper Midwest. And he got to eat her meat pies and doughnuts until the day he died. Across the peninsula, my Grandma Pierce was forever perfecting another variation of the meat pie, the Cornish pasty, mainstay of those Celtic immigrant ancestors who worked the iron and copper mines in the upper peninsula of Michigan. Both of my grandmothers used lard for their crusts; Grandma Pierce laid an egg on top of the filling of flank steak, potato, carrot, onion, and rutabaga before she sealed it all in a half-moon pastry jacket. Both of my grandmothers wore aprons all day and polished their silverware regularly.

When I think of housework, everything comes back to my grandmothers, mother, and aunts and laundry and meat pies and pasties: my grandmothers hanging clothes while the meat pies cooled on their kitchen windowsills, top crusts slit to release the fragrant steam. My mother and aunts hanging their own families' clothes while they baked their own updated versions of meat pies and pasties, almost as delicious without the lard. When I think of housework, I hear the music of their talk, the rise and fall of their laughter.

The meat pie steam of being alive.

When I actually *do* housework, however, I am usually unhappy, resentful, and ticked off at my husband, who is always upstairs working on . . . *something important*. Almost all of our arguments have to do with household chores — not the chores themselves as much as what my having to ask implies: that I am in charge of the trivial, that "nagging" is an acknowledgment of the trivial, that the trivial can always be postponed. If I mention the maze of cobwebs hovering over the maze of boxes of junk in our basement, for example, he will first turn to look at me incredulously, as if I have asked him to fork over a kidney or accompany me to high mass, and then let go his litany of priorities. He always agrees to do any chore I assign him, providing he can do it at his convenience and on his own terms. He will get the crumbs and slime off the kitchen floor, but he will do so with a damp paper towel rather than a Swiffer. (More infuriating is that it takes him five minutes and the floor is immaculate when he is finished.) He will vacuum the cat hair off the stairs, but exactly when he will do so is his ultrasecret mystery time, and by the time the planets have lined up correctly, we usually have a new cat in the house. "In May" is his standard answer when asked when the yard waste bagged the June before will be hauled to the brush dump. "In May," when his classes and meetings are over.

When Ruth Schwartz Cowan's *More Work for Mother: The Ironies of Household Technology from the Open Hearth to the Microwave* appeared in 1983, I was not yet thirty, had not yet married, had not yet "set up housekeeping," as my parents used to call it. Now I don't know how I got along without a dishwasher. I finally got one when I was thirty-seven, the year after I married, the same year I got my own washer and dryer and garbage disposal. What was it about marriage that necessitated the procurement of this host of timesaving household appliances? I never thought to ask until now. In one photograph taken at my wedding shower in 1990, I am lifting a new frying pan from a wad of pink tissue and smiling toward the camera. I am a *career woman*, a poet, a feminist, the least likely woman in my extended family to have (finally) married. It's a genuine smile; I am very happy, this is an excellent brand of cookware, a brand I'd never have owned as a single woman. But why not? What did the tribe know that I had yet to learn?

Cowan's book shatters the myth that American housewives' jobs have been simplified by vacuum cleaners, electric ovens, and washing machines since their inventions. What time these appliances saved, she points out, is now absorbed by lists of tasks just as absorbing. In "Less Work for Mother?" a 1987 spinoff essay, Cowan reiterates her claim that despite the so-called "industrial revolution in the home" that is said to have occurred from 1920 to 1960 due to the introduction of timesaving household appliances, "the average American housewife [of the following three decades] performed fifty to sixty hours of unpaid work in her home every week . . . now armed with dozens of motors and thousands of electronic chips . . . while working housewives logged thirty-five hours — virtually the equivalent of another full-time job." In *Never Done*, Susan Strasser talks about the evolution of the laundry task, saying that "over the long run, the automatic washer probably restructured rather than reduced laundry time" because "it changed the laundry pile from a weekly nightmare to an unending task . . . which was now spread out over the week." Ruth Cowan goes on to explore the ramifications of the automobile's present role in housework and concludes: "She may be exhausted at the end of her double day, but the modern 'working' housewife can at least fall into bed knowing that her efforts have made it possible to sustain her family at a level of health and comfort that not so long ago was reserved for the very rich."

Unlike most of my female colleagues who work both inside and outside their houses I am childless; I have only two people to clean up after. And I have to acknowledge that my husband cheerfully takes care of the cats and the trash without being asked to do so. I also need to reveal that for the last six years my secret weapon has been a red-haired housekeeping goddess named Yvonne, who comes over once or twice a month to help me wash floors, dust, and vacuum. Weekend mornings before the days of Yvonne, I fumed in my mother's housework uniform — a long T-shirt and underpants — blasting the music of angry women rockers and cursing when the vacuum cord strained out of the socket and shut the operation down. "They seem such a waste — / these days I barely remember — doing the work that has no / meaning, the work that will whirl on above me when my body / has crossed its arms to everything," laments Faith Shearin's speaker in "The Sinking." In other poems here, the household landscape seems infused with a similar grief. Gail Martin's speaker in "Lemons" gets tears in her eyes "seeing vinegar / and oil refuse to mix" and fills with sadness at the sight of lemons "stacked in a white bowl." Martha Rhodes's soupmaker waits "for one person / hungry enough to come home," and Joyce Sutphen's "Household Muse" "nurse[s] some fretful sorrow" in the throes of a housework binge.

But yesterday I hung out the season's first wash and watched with satisfaction from the back porch as it waved in the first warm currents of a midwestern spring. Our king-size cotton sheets, flags of the country of lavender blue. *Once I asked myself, when was I happy?* The fluffy cotton towels, my husband's ripe and holey workout clothes. *When did the light hold me and I didn't struggle?* My semiscandalous underwire bras pinned to the inside line, their satin cups full of wind, alongside my husband's briefs. Is this what it means to be content — the tulips and daffodils nudging through their green jackets, the purple finches and the waving sheets, all this useless beauty? On some days, yes. But most days I'm like the speaker in Allison Joseph's "Plenty," who wanders through a fabric store touching the bolts of fabric, thinking "of all the things that can be made / from these yards and yards of cloth, / the combinations infinite as long / as the shears are sharp, pincushions full."

There is no end to what women can make of their lives. We are, at our very core, pioneers, revolutionaries, and inventors as well as life-givers and nurturers. Out of the cast-off scraps of cloth, we make the quilts; out of the leftover meat and bruised vegetables, we conjure the nourishing stews. "My fingers are forks, my tongue is a rose . . . / I turn silver spoons into rabbit stew / make quinces my thorny upholstery . . . / how else could the side of beef walk / with the sea urchin roe?" sings the cook in Natasha Sajé's ode to kitchen alchemy.

In its purest form, even bitterness, like concentrated drops of almond and vanilla, can be charmed into everyday use. "I love the notion that we can take our most poisonous angers, our most despairing or humiliating or stalemated moments, and make something good of them — something tensile and enduring," says poet Leslie Ullman. Whether we are fully present in our tasks or "gone in the motion" of performing them, whether our stovetops are home to "stewpots of discontent" or Grandmother's favorite jam, something is always cooking.

"The female seer will burn upon this pyre"

ELIZABETH ALEXANDER

Sylvia Plath is setting my hair
on rollers made from orange-juice cans.
The hairdo is shaped like a pyre.

My locks are improbably long.
A pyramid of lemons somehow
balances on the rickety table

where we sit, in the rented kitchen
which smells of singed naps and bergamot.
Sylvia Plath is surprisingly adept

at rolling my unruly hair.
She knows how to pull it tight.
                              Few words.
Her flat, American belly,

her breasts in a twin sweater set,
stack of typed poems on her desk,
envelopes stamped to go by the door,

a freshly baked poppyseed cake,
kitchen safety matches, black-eyed Susans
in a cobalt jelly jar. She speaks a word,

"immolate," then a single sentence
of prophecy. The hairdo done,
the nursery tidy, the floor swept clean

of burnt hair and bumblebee husks.

How I Learned to Sweep

JULIA ALVAREZ

My mother never taught me sweeping . . .
One afternoon she found me watching
t.v. She eyed the dusty floor
boldly, and put a broom before
me, and said she'd like to be able
to eat her dinner off that table,
and nodded at my feet, then left.
I knew right off what she expected
and went at it. I stepped and swept;
the t.v. blared the news; I kept
my mind on what I had to do,
until in minutes, I was through.
Her floor was as immaculate
as a just-washed dinner plate.
I waited for her to return
and turned to watch the President,
live from the White House, talk of war:
in the Far East our soldiers were
landing in their helicopters
into jungles their propellors
swept like weeds seen underwater
while perplexing shots were fired
from those beautiful green gardens
into which these dragonflies
filled with little men descended.
I got up and swept again
as they fell out of the sky.
I swept all the harder when
I watched a dozen of them die . . .
as if their dust fell through the screen
upon the floor I had just cleaned.
She came back and turned the dial;
the screen went dark. *That's beautiful*,
she said, and ran her clean hand through
my hair, and on, over the window-

sill, coffee table, rocker, desk,
and held it up — I held my breath —
that's beautiful, she said, impressed,
she hadn't found a speck of death.

Down on My Knees

GINGER ANDREWS

cleaning out my refrigerator
and thinking about writing a religious poem
that somehow combines feeling sorry for myself
with ordinary praise, when my nephew stumbles in for coffee
to wash down what looks like a hangover
and get rid of what he calls hot dog water breath.
I wasn't going to bake the cake

now cooling on the counter, but I found a dozen eggs tipped
sideways in their carton behind a leftover Thanksgiving Jell-O dish.
There's something therapeutic about baking a devil's food cake,
whipping up that buttercream frosting,
knowing your sisters will drop by and say Lord yes
they'd love just a little piece.

Everybody suffers, wants to run away,
is broke after Christmas, stayed up too late
to make it to church Sunday morning. Everybody should

drink coffee with their nephews,
eat chocolate cake with their sisters, be thankful
and happy enough under a warm and unexpected January sun.

The Hurricane Sisters Work Regardless

GINGER ANDREWS

Scrubbing the upstairs tub at our first housecleaning job of the day,
I hate to whine about some trivial fever, chills and sore throat. Instead,
I decide to sing Old MacDonald Had a Farm, starting with the *E I E I O*,
to my oven-cleaning downstairs sister who has a large uterine tumor
and knows it won't get removed unless it becomes absolutely necessary.
She doesn't have insurance, and free clinic patients have to make do
with whatever surgeon volunteers, whenever there's time.

My diabetic sister, who hasn't had a slice of pie, a doughnut
or a cigarette in years, who watched me hog down half a bag
of miniature Snickers on the way to work, and might not believe
I could eat like that with a fever, who is dusting mini blinds
on the middle-floor windows, while ignoring the nasty body aches
resulting from Wednesday's flu shot, joins in on the *moo-moo's here,
moo-moo's there.*

Also scrubbing a tub, my basement sister, who's on her second round
of antibiotics for her third sinus infection of the year, hollers
up the stairway, *here a moo, there a moo.*

My lungs full of Lysol Basin Tub & Tile cleaner, I'm hacking
on the *quack-quacks* when my oven-cleaning sister,
now singing along, says, Hey, are you all right up there?

5

Romantic

MARGARET ATWOOD

Men and their mournful romanticisms
that can't get the dishes done —
that's freedom, that broken wineglass
in the cold fireplace.

When women wash underpants, it's a chore.
When men do it, an intriguing affliction.
How plangent, the damp socks flapping on the line,
how lost and single in the orphaning air . . .

She cherishes that sadness,
tells him to lie down on the grass,
closes each of his eyes with a finger,
applies her body like a poultice.

You poor thing, said the Australian woman
while he held our baby —
as if I had forced him to do it,
as if I had my high heel in his face.

Still, who's taken in?
Every time?
Us, and our empty hands, the hands
of starving nurses.

It's bullet holes we want to see in their skin,
scars, and the chance to touch them.

Kitchens: 1959

JULIANNA BAGGOTT

The year Nixon showed up in Moscow
in front of Macy's Model Kitchen and finger-poked

Khrushchev's broad chest, my mother lost her first baby.
Russians crowded the railed-off kitchen,

a display of modern American living.
Imagine the potato-and-onion smell of so many wool coats,

the cupboard hanging open to show off shelf space,
the box of S.O.S. ready to scrub it all down.

When Khrushchev says to Nixon in his husky Russian tongue,
Go fuck my grandmother, Elliot Erwitt translates the street talk,

shoots frame after frame that I'll find later in a book:
two angry men and the kitchen so small and tidy, I can only think

of my mother's first kitchen, her view the same as Erwitt's
if she'd been sitting at the breakfast table

in the garage apartment on Fernwood Street in Portsmouth,
a military town where they roll the mattresses

up on the beds because of the bugs,
but this one's not bad: a ceramic sink,

a Frigidaire, and a Hot Point stove for $75 a month.
My father's in his last year of duty,

the Russians are winning the final frontier,
and the A-bomb could drop from the sky

and melt every house on Fernwood Street,
but for now my mother is puffy and pale.

The bleeding started fast, the tiny child
lost in it somewhere — she never saw

what she'd imagined: arms, legs, her own small face —
and now days later, she shuffles to the cold stove.

It's on the blink, a wire coil model;
one little wire overheated and the whole thing shut down.

She turns it off, reaches in, fingers the wires,
twist-ties them. She's got a meat loaf

from a neighbor on the counter.
In a week or two she'll see the campaign poster

at the grocery store, Nixon and Khrushchev chin to chin.
She'll vote for Nixon, thinking maybe one day

his toughness will save her, her husband,
the small cluster of eggs inside her.

But she has already begun to doubt things.
She thinks nothing is truly reliable, not her body,

not this easy American life. She starts up the oven,
and as the wires solder themselves,

my mother smells smoke; something small is burning.

Poetry Despises Your Attempts at Domesticity

JULIANNA BAGGOTT

The vacuum's one lung stiffens, aged,
it puffs too tightly.
        It needs rest, Poetry says.
God bless her insistence: Ignore your aunts,
their plumage, their hospital corners, bleached
toilet bowls. The house aches. It has no gleaming
underside. It wants you to see it
for what it is, not for what it needs.
        And what is it? You've forgotten.
A collection of smeared prints, the daily rigor
of staying, a blessing of dust.
And now you remember what the house was to you
as a child: a giant full-skirted woman, it gathered you in,
squatted like a nesting bird, loved you with its hovering vigilance.
And you loved it, heated duct work, squealing pipes,
because it could always stand, walk away, revealing you
and your family for what you are,
a knot, huddled, bare,
        a circle of pale backs turned to the cold.

In Waking Words

DOROTHY BARRESI

for instance, for instance
My mother asleep at the kitchen table
is a commuter except
she is already at home, at work.
Her cheek skims a basket of married socks,
gold toe, green toe, heel and toe,
and I am tapdancing in her big belly, my hands
making S-shapes in the water.
Also brothers orbit there, or the idea of them
encoded, little sputniks.

But who wound the pets up so tight?
It is the fifties, the suburbs. Asleep,
the dog with pink lips and the cat with black lips
twitch on cold linoleum.
The refrigerator is so turquoise it hurts.
And this, too, you'll recognize
if I tell it right.
A child hit by a joyriding Caddy, circa fins,
is suddenly bounceable, laughing,
and because this is a dream,
thrown clear to the female grass.

What my mother wouldn't give
to have that dream again.
What I wouldn't give to have it for her.
But chaos demands space, and things lost
have a life of their own
long after we've stopped searching.

On her stove, a black-and-white flecked tea kettle
is whistling *here lies,*
ready to melt down onto the burner
and become event: metal, gone stars.

The Prodigal Daughter

DOROTHY BARRESI

If a daughter bent on pleasing
turns her knives
inward, then the salad plate goes

to the left of the glassware,
the cup aligned
with the soup spoon — where were we? Oh, yes,

the prodigal daughter
did not return.
She never left home in the first place.

And if the fatted lamb is brought to the spit & fire
in her honor,
his black head split jowl to jowl

so that the jewels of his brain
are sizzling, for pudding,
the snout a gourd scooped out

for pomegranate wine,
then she has made that dinner
and that unending drama.

In the gray hierarchy of cook smoke,
let her symbols go up:
ash and amaranth,

the ankle bracelet off at the stump.
This is not the story
of the water in the well,

but of the dutiful woman who might throw herself
down any moment
just to hear the splash,

then refrains. (Refrain)
This is not the new dispensation.
This is not the different earth.

Her old mother is crazy; she's smearing
roast garlic on her cheeks and reading
the riot act to the chickens

with a paring knife.
Her father? He's not gone yet, but he *needs*
her so—who will take care of him

in his early retirement?
Mutiny. Even the least fallen angels
take a dive sometimes. But that

she will not do.
There are dishes to do, and bread
to pound senseless, and dancing classes, and all those

damn sparks to contend with
around the fire pit
clicking its castanets. So what if she caught fire?

What if she who gave herself away so lavishly
in the interest of others
were sent up in a whippet of smoke

to signal the tribes: here is a woman
who was granted the mastery
of one thing, herself,

good-bye!
Outside, the road lays down
its dusty hammer and tongs,

field mice nest in the skulls of wolves,
and worms eat their way toward God
through dirt, or vice versa.

But who is this woman of blank hosannahs,
this genteel, wellborn
woman bound by pity or mercy or self-spite

to spin at the wall, plotting: and who, in any case,
will protect her if she leaves
from all the prodigal sons hitchhiking

like so much unclaimed freight by the side of the road,
sticking out their spoiled thumbs?
They have a lot of living to do

before they settle down
and marry that
cute thing next door, this

dervish in suspense, in tears.
Quick, someone sing a cheery song
about disgrace

and many veils.
Someone count the silverware.

Modern Love

JAN BEATTY

Early evening, five minutes before
you're due home, I slam the dishes
in the dishwasher, squeeze rivers
of 409 onto the kitchen floor and
counters, smear it white with too many
paper towels, check the clock, listen
for the doorbell of your arriving —
Love, this is not my dreamscape
my answer to romance's longing — but Love,
still I grab old food from the refrigerator
and sail it into the trash, call for
take-out with the breathy voice of
a woman in want — burritos again,
with enough jalapeño to make our eyes
water; Strange new world this shape
of our love: the details of our lives
stacked in piles of tabloids, month-
old pretzels in their lonely bag, and yes,
the paint peeling off the porch since spring,
no time now to wash the clothes. I do
the only thing a woman in love can:
clear papers off the bed with a wide sweep,
slide in the video, pour the soft drinks,
so we can eat in our element, our little city;
so we can tear open time to find the heart,
heart enough for us to fill our bellies and
fill our bodies with each other until
we surface to ourselves again, until we're
the only ones here tonight, and the look
in your eyes looking at me is the beautiful
sight, and my only complaints are two:
that I didn't make myself ready
for you sooner in life, that
I can't give better,
love you more.

Pittsburgh Poem

JAN BEATTY

On Sarah Street on the South Side,
the old woman still stands with her broom, imagining
the air full of lug and swish from the steelworker's boot,
armies of gray lunchbuckets grace her thoughts
as she sweeps with the part of her that still believes;
sweeps while her sister makes paska and horseradish with red beets,
sweeps away the stains of a dead husband and a disappointing daughter.

She thinks of the dark well of J & L, how it sifted down to nothing,
the mill's hole of a mouth that ate full years of her life,
nights she pulled her husband from Yarsky's bar across the street,
him smiling like a bagful of dimes, half a paycheck spent,
the whole time soot covering their clothes, the car, the windowsills,
like disease, someone else's hands.

She holds tight onto the good times, the new green velour couch,
Saturday walks to the Markethouse for fresh red cabbage and greens,
trips to the Brown & Green store for new T-shirts, South Side windows
brimming taffeta and satin on the way to Mass at St. Michael's,
when the world was gleaming and available for one glorious day.

Now shadows angle across her print housedress and she holds tight
to her broom, hears her sister primping in the kitchen, smells the pea soup
with sauerkraut, the homemade mushroom gravy for perogies, she thinks
of the ten years since her husband died, of her daughter who calls
on holidays, she stands on her concrete lawn,
taking care of something invisible, the listless air,
her life.

Dictionary for the New Century

KIMBERLY BLAESER

What would *housework* mean
to women who haul water from springs,
use lye soap and scrub boards,
who hang flypaper on ceilings
and sew cloth cupboard curtains
on the family treadle machine?

What does *kitchen appliance* mean
to those toasting bread in ovens
of old wood stoves,
or *bathroom appliance*
to those donning snow boots
to walk to the outhouse?

Somewhere between microwave pancakes
and the *state-of-the-art* mixmaster
I trip over the kitchen slop pail
retch at the smell of lard rendering.
Just as my fingers settle on the DVD remote
I remember to empty the ashcan.

At three my daughter kisses and releases her fish
at four she asks if a chicken is a dead bird.
At forty like Billy Pilgrim I come unstuck in time
still wait to take my turn in a three-foot washtub,
then light candles and soak in a warm whirlpool
now camped uneasily between *progress* and *nostalgia*.

With a heavy-duty vacuum and a lightweight canister
I cruise the air-conditioned floors of my house
sweep away unearned *guilt* or hire a cleaning lady.
With electric everything and my computer whirring
I *work* my way through memories and philosophies
try to recollect that proverb about idle hands.

What does *convenience* mean in a country of prosperity?
Should we use or release our histories?
Can *education* repay old debts?
If *science* and *technology* are the answers
who have we hired to ask the questions?
And what was it you said about *women's work*?

What They Did by Lamplight

KIMBERLY BLAESER

Clean rice, handstitch
make pies, roll jingles
patch jeans, shake dice
clean fish, roll cigarettes
read from *The Farmer.*
Braid rugs, mend nets, tell stories
write letters, bead, cut quilt squares
boil swamp tea, deliver their babies.
Darn socks, peel potatoes, drink coffee
shuffle cards, cut hair, can tomatoes
sift flour, bead, sing church songs.
Scrub socks, gossip.
sing country songs
make tobacco ties
braid sweet grass
prepare their dead.
Beat frosting
laugh
embroider
crack nuts
depill sweaters
wipe their tears.
Search penny jar for old coins
shell peas, cut birchbark patterns
thread matching buttons together.
Build fire, make soap, join their hands
knead bread, read seed catalogues, smoke
slice apples, squeeze color into margarine.
Change diapers, shuck corn, soak beans
rock their children, boil water, crochet doilies
clean sunflower seeds, can dill pickles.
Sharpen knives, eat, iron
dance together
nurse their babies
remember their dead.

Sewing

MARIANNE BORUCH

My mother was sewing: pajamas for us, always,
and curtains for the window
to sleep in. At night she pulled them loose
against the wide backyard where the dog
roamed from plum tree to willow, where
the hammock hung in shade.

But all of it was shade at night
except the moon's full face.
Small umbrellas on my flannel, small
pirates on my brother's as if in dreams
it rained too much
and enough ships docked there
for a whole childhood's worth of thieves.

Years, the same room, the same window.
My brother's bed there, and my bed there.
And arguments between us like a wheel
turned to make the other go,
as through one engine.

In the dark, I heard her sewing. Each stitch
a splinter put back and back so rapidly.
Not song exactly. Not pain.
It's the little wizard wayward spool I still
think about, high
and quick — the way it almost
flew, but turned to make and make.

Cooking Catalogue

JILL BRECKENRIDGE

On a cool September day, the soup commences:
vegetable beef, its vitamins an orange and green
rainbow, its sky dotted with beef, the dark
storms of carnivores. Then split peas, solidly
green or yellow all the way through. I soak them,
boil them until they give their sandy gift,
wrapped in ham smoke and salt. And turkey noodle:
breaking the empty carcass, boiling it,
dark meat and white relaxing from the dancing bones.
My kitchen a smorgasbord of smells, I ladle
steaming soup into seven bowls. At the table,
six people take and eat, while I lean back, full,
and watch an early snow stir and blow outside.

When lilacs unlock their buds, it's salad time:
tuna salad, celery a crisp parenthesis
around slipshod macaroni. Radishes snapping
back at the bite; thin cucumber wheels and purple
onions roll me away in shivers; boiled eggs
gussied up with mustard and green chives. And artichoke,
the queen of vegetables, the sharp-tongued ruler.
Green crown shined and oiled, her layered
wisdom begins with justice only but ends with mercy
and butter melted and lemon mayonnaise.
Oh the feast of it all! Oh spring!
Pass the salad, pass the iced tea,
pass the lilacs for a second smell.

Desert Flowers

JEANNE BRYNER

Their men took them to flat-footed milltowns.
Soft, doe-eyed mountain women and daisy haired
hillgirls said good-bye to their Mama's
wood-stove kitchen, their Daddy's clover fields,
and having babies at home.

Women who painted with needles said good-bye
to their granny's quilt frame. Hands that sliced
peaches and dishpans full of green beans
left blue canning jars — clean and silent —
in rows on cellar floors.

Their men said there was no fit place
for summer gardens, and these hillwomen hoped
there'd be a patch for tulips, prayed
there'd be a spot for apple trees.

When they came, the houses were shoe boxes,
air smelled worse than dirty sock haystacks,
iddy-biddy yards were cages where children
paced like tiger cubs, and cars were fleas
on the back of skinny, gray dog roads.

Our mothers were saguaro cacti
learning to live without dancing clear streams
rushing down crying purple mountains, learning
to accept the mill's lattice of steel cables
and its menagerie of mercury men.

Our mothers were saguaro cacti
knowing they must turn brown to conserve water
so we, their daughters, could bloom.

Forty years later, we are their first arm.
Our daughters will be their second arm.
As both arms curve toward the breathless stars,
we will bury the placentas of their great-grandchildren
in the hills. We will give thanks to these beautiful women
who learned to survive the drought.

Part of a Larger Country

JEANNE BRYNER

Morning sun cradles a bowl of apples,
my table stammers as I shove
it away from the stove's clean face.
Who am I? — the sleepy innkeeper,
red bandanna and dance partner broom,
oceans of broken Cheerios,
dog hair, mown grass sifted over
dappled floor patterns.

Mountains of hungry years
swept and thrown away,
sand and pebbles, crumbs
and grit, equalization's found
when tilling flat places
which are part of a larger country.

Ladder-back chairs carried
to the hallway's scarred tunnel,
jelly handprints, blue crayon graffiti.
My children race to each seat
yelling *Choo-choo, All aboard.*

In the busy land of pretend,
maybe I am the conductor
smiling in rubber gloves, taking tickets,
orders for graham crackers, cold milk.
While they ride imagination's trail
across sheltered tracks, my string mop
swirls and chokes, her clay hair
floats a vein of hot sudsy water.

How easily balloons travel, how fast
carousels twirl. Dumping sludge buckets
week after week, I wonder, which smoky
factory will steal their singing voice?

Night paints the quick faces of passengers,
families behind love's stained glass,
the faith and duty of water and dirt,
one helix of what holds us together,
how the moon must eat her heart to bloom.

Five-Year Plan

VICTORIA CHANG

A good Chinese American housewife has a five-year plan.
It's strategic, sparse,

menacing. It stutters at nothing, a tin present tense, perhaps
a new VCR

in two years. A good Chinese American daughter washes
windows and retains

curvatures. And when I'm finished, I revise my five-year plan
to exclude window-

washing, to include speaker of the house in two years, in four,
maybe president.

And a good Chinese daughter and housewife has a ten-year plan,
but the sum of parts

does not equal the whole. And when did this dimming and mapping
start? When did kicking

apart and putting back together tread? At birth, a contract
must occur, because

all Chinese parents ask new son-in-laws: *Do you have pension?*
And it's reinforced,

the way a rubber snake sneaks and scares. It's not amazing that
we can balance eggs

on our heads and fix a man's heart together. We have degrees
in everything and

nothing. We can polish cats while solving proofs, like belching &
breathing. And all this

premeditation, like sugar in theory, but really tastes
aluminum, clogs

the esophagus. It always grows back, never reaches twenty-
twenty and there is

no standard deviation, no chance for seeing a spare owl
or the red fox that

wanders just beyond the border. All knew I would "make it," or
at least control it

to a strangle so that the throat only brings in half the air.

The Floral Apron

MARILYN CHIN

The woman wore a floral apron around her neck,
that woman from my mother's village
with a sharp cleaver in her hand.
She said, "What shall we cook tonight?
Perhaps these six tiny squid
lined up so perfectly on the block?"

She wiped her hand on the apron,
pierced the blade into the first.
There was no resistance,
no blood, only cartilage
soft as a child's nose. A last
iota of ink made us wince.

Suddenly, the aroma of ginger and scallion fogged our senses,
and we absolved her for that moment's barbarism.
Then, she, an elder of the tribe,
without formal headdress, without elegance,
deigned to teach the younger
about the Asian plight.

And although we have traveled far
we would never forget that primal lesson
— on patience, courage, forbearance,
on how to love squid despite squid,
how to honor the village, the tribe,
that floral apron.

A Man in My Bed Like Cracker Crumbs

SANDRA CISNEROS

I've stripped the bed.
Shaken the sheets and slumped
those fat pillows like tired tongues
out the window for air and sun
to get to. I've let

the mattress lounge in
its blue-striped dressing gown.
I've punched and fluffed.
All morning. I've billowed and snapped.
Said my prayers to *la Virgen de la Soledad*
and now I can sit down
to my typewriter and cup
because she's answered me.

Coffee's good.
Dust motes somersault and spin.
House clean.
I'm alone again.
Amen.

quilting

LUCILLE CLIFTON

somewhere in the unknown world
a yellow eyed woman
sits with her daughter
quilting.

some other where
alchemists mumble over pots.
their chemistry stirs
into science. their science
freezes into stone.

in the unknown world
the woman
threading together her need
and her needle
nods toward the smiling girl
remember
this will keep us warm.

how does this poem end?
    do the daughters' daughters quilt?
    do the alchemists practice their tables?
    do the worlds continue spinning
    away from each other forever?

Mother, a Young Wife Learns to Sew

GERALDINE CONNOLLY

Those were the days
she slipped a silver needle
neat as a minnow
through a piece of cloth.

It went swimming
up and out
of the river of fabric
guided by her hand.

Was that glance up
at the open window
a happy gaze, or a cry
to be outside, running, free

through carpets of garnet
vines or azalea blaze,
not pushing the steel point
of an instrument through linen,

not putting hooks and loops
and buttonholes in order,
staying to the task, keeping on,
baste and stitch, as the world burned
and glittered and she held on
to purpose and industry.

New House

GERALDINE CONNOLLY

There's always the illusion the museum I carry
inside me, of coal dust, black bread and worn-out brooms
could turn into a seaside palazzo of framed lithographs
and immaculate linens. There's the hope that some magical
storm could sweep over my life, making dinners prepare
themselves, dust motes fly back into the atmosphere,
newspapers slide out of their messy heaps into trash bins.

My marriage, too, could evolve like that dream
where I grow wings and fly through sun-filled windows
into the arms of a beautiful stranger. We two will
sit back in a chaise longue in freshly painted harmony,
tend hothouse orchids on the patio and photograph
street-sweepers at dawn. We will witness glorious sunsets
behind the Pillars of Hercules reconstructed on our lawn.
There will be no weeds, smudged windows or carpenter ants,
no growling dogs or nosy neighbors with garish swing sets.

I will indulge my desire for a Moroccan bathroom
with marble floors and a mosaic dragon. It's not that
I can't see that a fresh start is a white lie, my dream
of arriving at a fulcrum of elegance just another decorative
hope embellished with gold braid. The truth is I will
never get around to painting that dining room mural
or hanging linen swags. My success is of no consequence
to these walls. This ceiling fan could be the one I die beneath.
But I move past misgiving and chaos with chipped
stoneware, tattered baggage and dreamy optimism,
the throb of salvation beating in my chest like a drum.

Grating Parmesan

BARBARA CROOKER

A winter evening,
sky, the color of cobalt,
the night coming down like the lid on a pot.
On the stove, the ghosts of summer simmer:
tomatoes, garlic, basil, oregano.
Steam from the kettle rises,
wreathes the windows.
You come running when I reach for the grater,
"Help me?" you ask, reversing the pronouns,
part of your mind's disordered scramble.
Together, we hold the rind of the cheese,
scrape our knuckles on the metal teeth.
A fresh pungency enters the room.
You put your fingers in the fallen crumbs:
"Snow," you proudly exclaim, and look at me.
Three years old, nearly mute,
but master of metaphor.
Most of the time, we speak without words.

Outside, the icy stones in the sky
glitter in their random order.
It's a night so cold, the very air freezes flesh,
a knife in the lungs, wind rushing
over the coil of the planet
straight from Siberia,
a high howl from the wolves of the steppes.
As we grate and grate, the drift rises higher.
When the family gathers together,
puts pasta in their bowls,
ladles on the simmered sauce,
you will bless each one
with a wave of your spoon:
"Snowflakes falling all around."
You're the weatherman
of the kitchen table.

And, light as a feather,
the parmesan sprinkles down,
its newly fallen snow
gracing each plate.

Broom

DEBORAH DIGGES

More than my sixteen rented houses and their eighty or so rooms
held up by stone or cinderblock foundations,
most facing north, with useless basements,
wrought iron fences to the curb,
beat-up black mailboxes —
eagles impaled through breasts to edifice —
or set like lighthouses
some distance from the stoop a thousand miles inland,

or close enough to sea the sea gulls
settled mornings in the playing fields I passed
on this continent and others
as I walked my sons to school or to the train —

more than the kitchen door frames where is carved the progress
of their growth, one then the other on his birthday
backed against a wall, almost on tiptoe —

and more than the ruler
I have laid across their skulls
where the older's brown hair like my own,
or the younger's blond like his father's, covered abundantly
what was once only a swatch of scalp
I'd touch as they slept to know their hearts beat —

more than the height at which, and in this house,
the markings stopped like stairs leading to ground level,
and they walked out into the world,
dogged, no doubt, by the ghost of the man, their father,
and the men who tried to be their fathers,
father their wildness —

and more, even, than the high sashed windows
and windows sliding sideways
through which I watched for them, sometimes squinting,
sometimes through my hands cupped on cold glass
trying to see in the dark my men approaching,
my breath blinding me,
the first born surely the man I would have married,
the second, me in his man's body —

more than the locks left open and the creaking steps,
the books left open like mirrors on the floor
and the sinks where we washed our faces
and the beds above which our threefold dreams collided,

I have loved the broom I took into my hands
and crossed the threshold to begin again,
whose straw I wore to nothing,
whose shaft I could use to straighten a tree, or break
across my knee to kindle the first winter fire,
or use to stir the fire,

broom whose stave is pine or hickory,
and whose skirt of birch-spray and heather
offers itself up as nest matter,
arcs like the equator
in the corner, could we see far enough,
or is parted one way like my hair.

Once I asked myself, when was I happy?
I was looking at a February sky.
When did the light hold me and I didn't struggle?
And it came to me, an image
of myself in a doorway, a broom in my hand,
sweeping out beach sand, salt, soot,
pollen and pine needles, the last December leaves,
and mud wasps, moths, flies crushed to wafers,
and spring's first seed husks,
and then the final tufts like down, and red bud petals
like autumn leaves — so many petals —

sweeping out the soil the boys tracked in
from burying in the new yard another animal —
broom leaving intact the spiders' webs,
careful of those,
and careful when I danced with the broom,
that no one was watching,
and when I hacked at the floor
with the broom like an axe, jammed handle through glass
as if the house were burning and I must abandon ship
as I wept over a man's faithlessness, or wept over my own —

and so the broom became
an oar that parted waters, raft-keel and mast, or twirled
around and around on the back lawn,
a sort of compass through whose blurred counter-motion
the woods became a gathering of brooms,
onlooking or ancestral.

I thought I could grow old here,
safe among the ghosts, each welcomed,
yes, welcomed back for once, into this house, these rooms

in which I have got down on hands and knees and swept my hair
across my two sons' broad tan backs,
and swept my hair across you, swinging my head,
lost in the motion,
lost swaying up and down the whole length of your body,
my hair tangling in your hair,
our hair matted with sweat and my own cum, and semen,
lost swaying, smelling you,
smelling you humming,
gone in the motion, back and forth, sweeping.

The Size of a Bed Sheet

AMY DRYANSKY

A woman sits back on her heels.
Alone by a deep, green river,
she washes a brightly colored cloth
the size of a bed sheet.
It tugs at her hands, twists downstream
but she holds on, winding it in
to rub against the rocks, releasing it
to unfurl beneath the water.
The woman is lost in the rhythm of her work
and remembering the life of the cloth.
She ticks off on imaginary fingers
the special occasions of its use:
when she had to pack all she owned in an hour
and move deeper into the hills.
As a tent when she had no other shelter.
To make one room into two when her children got older.
As a shroud for her husband.
As a shroud for her son.
She thinks again how lucky she was to get it,
how rare: a piece so big without any holes.

The Ugly Step Sister

DENISE DUHAMEL

You don't know what it was like.
My mother marries this bum who takes off on us,
after only a few months, leaving his little Cinderella
behind. Oh yes, Cindy will try to tell you
that her father died. She's like that, she's a martyr.
But between you and me, he took up
with a dame close to Cindy's age.
My mother never got a cent out of him
for child support. So that explains
why sometimes the old lady was gruff.
My sisters and I didn't mind Cindy at first,
but her relentless cheeriness soon took its toll.
She dragged the dirty clothes to one of Chelsea's
many laundromats. She was fond of talking
to mice and rats on the way. She loved doing dishes
and scrubbing walls, taking phone messages,
and cleaning toilet bowls. You know,
the kind of woman that makes the rest
of us look bad. My sisters and I
weren't paranoid, but we couldn't help
but see this manic love for housework
as part of Cindy's sinister plan. Our dates
would come to pick us up and Cindy'd pop out
of the kitchen offering warm chocolate chip cookies.
Critics often point to the fact that my sisters and I
were dark and she was blond, implying
jealousy on our part. But let me
set the record straight. We have the empty bottles
of Clairol's Nice 'n Easy to prove
Cindy was a fake. She was what her shrink called
a master manipulator. She loved people
to feel bad for her — her favorite phrase was a faint,
"I don't mind. That's OK." We should have known
she'd marry Jeff Charming, the guy from our high school
who went on to trade bonds. Cindy finagled her way
into a private Christmas party on Wall Street,

charging a little black dress at Barney's
which she would have returned the next day
if Jeff hadn't fallen head over heels.
She claimed he took her on a horse and buggy ride
through Central Park, that it was the most romantic
evening of her life, even though she was home
before midnight—a bit early, if you ask me, for Manhattan.
It turned out that Jeff was seeing someone else
and had to cover his tracks. But Cindy didn't
let little things like another woman's happiness
get in her way. She filled her glass slipper
with champagne she had lifted
from the Wall Street extravaganza. She toasted
to Mr. Charming's coming around, which he did
soon enough. At the wedding, some of Cindy's friends
looked at my sisters and me with pity. The bride insisted
that our bridesmaids' dresses should be pumpkin,
which is a hard enough color for anyone to carry off.
But let me assure you, we're all very happy
now that Cindy's moved uptown. We've
started a mail order business—cosmetics
and perfumes. Just between you and me,
there's quite a few bucks to be made
on women's self-doubts. And though
we don't like to gloat, we hear Cindy Charming
isn't doing her aerobics anymore. It's rumored
that she yells at the maid, then locks herself in her room,
pressing hot match tips into her palm.

Good Woman

HEID ERDRICH

The Good Woman's home makes up into beds:
pullouts that creak and plaid sofa-sleepers.
Piles of mongrel boys toss in every room,
strays with nowhere else to rest. She takes
them in, gives them each other, makes enough.

The Good Woman's screens all hang open,
or stand propped to beckon like a waved hand.
Her doors all stay unlatched, except one: behind it,
a high floral bed, or one plumped with geometrics,
and a broad or flat back she can curl her hips to,
or lock out, or leave alone.

The Good Woman's house or trailer or apartment
smells of the crockpot simmering bone and broth
and beans. It smells of foods that stretch to mouths
opening wider and wider every year.

The Good Woman wraps in wool and sits up before sun
on her porch or stoop or fire escape.
She smokes or takes tea hot or with a shot.
Across her lawn, across the street, down the sidewalk,
a path runs toward rail yard, bus station, truck stop:
all ways the boys leave, or find their way to her home.

The Good Woman holds out her hands to the blue dawn.
Beasts with heavy heads and twisting horns
bow down, breathe her in and sigh.
She has never known if this is a dream,
so she goes on waiting in the cold
for visitation, vision, benediction.

The Good Woman falls from another world, clutches
at roots and rocks and creatures as she tumbles.
Her hair rains over her face. She does not know time.
When she lands, in her pockets, in her hands,
all medicines, minerals, meat we will need,
all that the people must know to survive.

Sweeping Heaven

HEID ERDRICH

Someone has to sweep these million golden
steps to God's throne, but not for long.
Not since I swept aside some lapis clouds
and glimpsed in the swirl what shone
through heaven's great vaulted window —
the whirling, light-studded universe below.
All the years I've swept his throne, God never
said a word. Now this broom weighs
in my hands like stone. I hurl it down,
watch it shoot sparks of shattered glass
into the slow deep. My wings grow fiery,
sear me to their roots. Cold heaven cannot keep
such a molten soul — I cast myself out to plummet
on useless wings. My hair is a flaming comet, I burn
through countless atmospheres. Hurtling, contracting,
cooling to a blue-white, gem-hard point, I strike a hole
in the starry roof of a North Dakota night, and sink
through a girl's unblinking eye, and settle below her throat.
There I stretch, though my wings won't rest. They beat
hard in her chest until she feels swept through inside
by something restless, something opening so wide
it showers like the wheeling prairie sky.

Peonies

SUSAN FIRER

The young girls walk by looking like wedding
cakes, art nouveau vases. They are
wearing only peonies. Exhausted
from wearing beauty, they night hurry
home to pull the flowers over their heads.
They learn that once you wear
a dress of peonies, your skin is forever
fragranced with the flowers' operatic sweet sadness. All
over the early June city, collapsed dresses of peonies
still as rugs incense bedrooms. Wild
canaries fly from the dresses' peony-scented puddles
and sing about the sleeping girls.

Have you heard the peonies' glossolalia?
Have you ever watched a black swallowtail's
gold and sky-blue pierced wings rearranged
by 44 mph winds, while it holds
to a Festiva Maxima Blush peony,
all the while maintaining all
its delicate migrating strength?
Have you seen your neighbor,
white-nightgowned, stop
the morning of her death
to bring greedily to her
face one last time the fragrance
of her greatly loved white Le Jours?

Looking at the sleeping new-
born in its white bassinet, one
would never believe, even if told in great detail,
what will happen to that infant during its life.
Or, if one did believe, one might go mad
with fast forwarded beauty, boredom, and terror.
Looking at the tight small gumball bud, it is
difficult to imagine the coming unfurling,
the coming foliage, the slow-opening beauty,

the insane fragrance. I watch
the drunk crazy ants come like explorers
to travel the tight white and green globes,
the holy-trinity-leaved peony buds.

All over the city, around paint-chipped garages,
around perfectly painted garages,
separating lot lines,
tied to dooryard black-iron railings,
on pillowcases and beds,
holding up houses,
in vases surrounding baths,
in the convent's oddly upright manacled bunches,
in under birdbath heavy collapsed bunches,
in vacant lots, and
reflected in witching balls,
peonies bow with fragrance
and all such burdens of beauty.

It is not hard to understand why my
immigrant grandmothers, both
the tall elegant French one and
the sweet doughy Czechoslovakian one,
prized their Limoges and cut-
glass dishes and peonies equally,
why they carried to their American homes
the promise-heavy flowers,
why they opened the soil around their new
homes and planted all the sweet
possible peonies they could find sun for,
nor why when

my mother married and moved to the new
wilderness of the suburbs she
carried the newspaper-wrapped dream
peonies with her. And I,
second generation on each family side,
have planted double-flowered Longfellow peonies
and Mrs. Franklin D. Roosevelt peonies and
Avalanche peonies all along my front steps

just so that you June visiting
might breathe in all the flowers' information,
longevity, and mad medicinal genius.

My neighbor planted her entire front yard in peonies.
In June, I am disabled with the wild sweet smell.
I cannot sleep. Breathing in the peonies' fragrance
it is easy to understand why people wallpaper
their bedrooms with peonies, perfectly preserve
them under glass bells, try to replicate
their smell in perfumes & in house sprays,
and sleep under peony-decorated comforters.
No dreams are as wonderful as dreams
had after breathing in Queen of Hamburg peonies.
After I've breathed in nights of the truth-drug flowers,
ask me and I will tell you
about women's body memories, about
the slow, moist-opening
of peonies, the ruffled silk slippery dark-
red petals, the ant licked
open peonies, the wealthy smell of nights
of peonies that dream and swell, grow
from tightness to wild reckless
loud unfurled dropping petals.

Have you ever rubbed a peony petal
between your thumb and index finger?
It is smoother than magnolia
tongues, sweeter than yellow cake,
better than any Chinese potion.
Put a peony in your hair —
you will not be disappointed
with the suggestions whispered in your ear.

After the Miscarriage

DIANE GILLIAM FISHER

I spend my days knitting booties
to sell, I say, to the baby boutique
across our street. So I am here
often, in this back corner
of Woolworth's: cold metal handle
of a red plastic basket digging
into the soft crook of my arm as
I count out fuzzy paper-banded skeins
of pink, blue, yellow, green, white.
It makes sense to my arm, what I am doing.

Two grandmas push a brown, wobbly
cart down my aisle. They shuffle around
a bit, pick stuff up, put it back.
The short one looks at me in front
of the baby yarn. "This cotton yarn's
on sale, honey," she says. "You ever
make those old-timey dishrags?
You yarn-over to increase one stitch at each end
then knit a row even. Just keep going
like that till it's as big as you want
then switch: cast-off instead of the yarn-over.
Goes real fast, lotsa people like 'em.
They're good for scrubbing."

I look at the thin yarn for babies, think
how tight and hard it will twist
on my skinniest needles.
I walk down to where the old women are,
look at the fat cotton yarn.
I stand long after the grandmas have gone
and think how the thick cotton
slides easily off big needles, simple
as cast-on, cast-off. How it is good
for scrubbing, soaks up what has spilled
then wrings out dry and clean.
How maybe it will save me.

Sweet Hour

DIANE GILLIAM FISHER

And God wrought special miracles by the hands of Paul: So that from his body were brought unto the sick, handkerchiefs or aprons, and the diseases departed from them, and the evil spirits went out from them. Acts 19:11–12

Mama pulls the prayer-cloth
from the laundry basket. It's too small
to fold, but she smooths it
with both hands over the curve of her leg
before she lays it back in the Bible.
The early summer night sounds like frogs
taking over the whole warm world.
We've come to her room
to be alone, to sit on the bed, fold
laundry, tell secrets. We talk
to our dead and, yes, they listen.
Oh Mama, I'm so glad.

The prayer-cloth came to her
from Uncle Lou, who was a prayer
warrior. He anointed the hand-sized
square of muslin with oil
and prayed over it. It came
for her first cancer, now gone
with the breast, then came closer,
next to the lung now clean
and whole as the cloth.
This is authorized by scripture,
Mama says, from Saint Paul
who could not be in all places
at all times, and so dispensed pieces
of his clothing to do his work and God's.

It's mostly Daddy's workshirts
in the basket, some tube socks,
and a pair of my daughter's jeans
we had to wash
because she only brought one pair
and wore them down to the creek.
I pull them out last,
fold them in at the waist
and spread one hand flat to hold them
high against my chest
while my other hand smooths,
down as far as I can reach,
along their mysterious length.

Upper Peninsula Landscape with Aunts

PAMELA GEMIN

Home from casino or fish fry,
the aunts recline
in their sisters' dens,
kicking off canvas shoes
and tucking their nylon footies
inside, remarking
on each other's pointy toes
and freckled bunions.

When Action 2 News comes on
they shake their heads and *tsk tsk tsk*
and stroke their collarbones.
The aunts hold their shoulderstrap purses
tight into their hips
and double-check their back seats.
The last politician they trusted
was FDR, and only then
when he kept his pants on.

The aunts won't be dickered down,
they'll tell you *a buck is a buck*,
as they wash and rinse freezer bags,
scrape off aluminum foil.

The aunts know exciting ways
with government cheese,
have furnished trailer homes
with S&H green stamp lamps and Goodwill sofas;
brook trout and venison thaw
in their shining sinks.

With their mops and feather dusters
and buckets of paint on sale,
with their hot glue guns and staplers
and *friendly plastic* jewelry kits,
with their gallons of closeout furniture stripper,

the aunts are hurricanes who'll marbleize
the inside of your closets
before you've had time
to put coffee on.

The aunts are steam-powered, engine-driven,
early rising women of legendary
soap and water beauty
who've pushed dozens of screaming babies
out into this stolen land.
They take lip or guff from no man,
child, or woman; tangle with aunts
and they'll give you what for times six
and then some: don't *make* them come up those stairs!

And yes they are acquainted
with the Bogeyman,
his belly full of robbery and lies.
The aunts have aimed deer rifles
right between his eyes, dead-bolted him out
and set their dogs upon him,
or gone tavern to tavern to bring him home,
carried him down from his nightmare
with strong black tea, iced his split lips,
painted his fighting cuts with Mercurochrome.

And they have married Cornishmen and Swedes,
and other Irish, married their sons and daughters off
to Italians and Frenchmen and Finns;
buried their parents and husbands and each other,
buried their drowned and fevered and miscarried children;
turned grandchildren upside down
and shaken the swallowed coins loose
from their windpipes; ridden the whole wide world
on the shelves of their hips.

The aunts know paradise is born
from rows of red dirt, red coffee cans,
prayers for rain. Whenever you leave
their houses, you leave with pockets and totes
full of strawberry jam and rum butter balls
and stories that weave themselves into your hair.

Some have already gone to the sky
to make pasties and reorganize the cupboards.
The rest will lead camels
through needles' eyes
to the shimmering kingdom of Heaven.

Perhaps the World Ends Here

JOY HARJO

The world begins at a kitchen table. No matter what, we must eat to live.

The gifts of earth are brought and prepared, set on the table. So it has been since creation, and it will go on.

We chase chickens or dogs away from it. Babies teethe at the corners. They scrape their knees under it.

It is here that children are given instructions on what it means to be human. We make men at it, we make women.

At this table we gossip, recall enemies and the ghosts of lovers.

Our dreams drink coffee with us as they put their arms around our children. They laugh with us at our poor falling-down selves and as we put ourselves back together once again at the table.

The table has been a house in the rain, an umbrella in the sun.

Wars have begun and ended at this table. It is a place to hide in the shadow of terror. A place to celebrate the terrible victory.

We have given birth on this table, and have prepared our parents for burial here.

At this table we sing with joy, with sorrow. We pray of suffering and remorse. We give thanks.

Perhaps the world will end at the kitchen table, while we are laughing and crying, eating of the last sweet bite.

Feeding Frenzy

HOLLY IGLESIAS

1.

Domestic Ham: A Reverie

A time we rightfully called ours, when breakfast was toast, baloney lunch,
and dinner had several parts requiring knife and fork. Coffee only came in
coffee flavor. It was everywhere, a God-given right like freedom or cheap gas,
in a world of pork chops and pot roast, canned beans and beets, of Miracle
Whip and Tang and the bread called Wonder, white and free of shame,
in settlements blossoming — plots big and small: strip malls, patio slabs,
Disneyland — to the tune of CONELRAD's alert.

We were not a pasta people. We took our noodles as we took our potatoes,
with gravy, at a great distance from salads, which were suspect. Bacon our
king, fearing no yolk, we were strangers to tacos and pizza, ramen and
vinaigrette, to curry and salsa. Father refusing rice, Mother secretly craving
chop suey, our baby laughs gurgling through lips the telltale red of Hawaiian
Punch.

2.

The Birth of Ranch Dressing

The time for French had passed. Gone the iceberg coated in orange and
with it the Italian and the Russian, the Blue and the Thousand Island. Like
domestic astronauts, we were launched into new orbits, Mother mixing spice
packet with vinegar and oil in the Hidden Valley cruet, proclaiming, *It's
ranch. It's home-made.* What ranch, what state was left unsaid. We suspected
Nevada and worried at the thought of her in Western togs, perched on a split-
rail fence, flirting with a cowpoke while she awaited her divorce from our
father.

3.

Gelatin Mold

Newly wed, she twirled around the kitchen in Capri pants and ballerina
flats, a Camel smoking on the windowsill above appliances bedecked in
tiny clothes. She learned bluing and Bab-O, Melmac and bone china;

foods to fortify—clove-studded hams and scalloped potatoes—and to amuse—porcupine meatballs and pear halves impersonating sombreros. Lurking in her recipes, the despair and wit that cut through Dream-Whip fog.

Go-to-Devotions Rump Roast
Lazy Housewife Pickles
Impressive Desperation Dessert

In the years of aerosol cheese and miniature marshmallows, she lost me. Like others, I turned to the raw and fibrous, hungry for difficult grains, foreign porridge and dense bread. It's true: I left her to her airy mousses and standing rib roasts and screaming orange salad dressing. That delicate aspic quivering upon an inscrutable, empty table.

4.
Flop House

Figure he pushed away from the bar—*Seamy side of life, adio!*—fingers dimpling the red vinyl bumper—what? ten times? before he headed home—*Come on, honey, how's about a kiss?*—the Rusty Nails quieting the benzedrine buzz as he drove into the glare of a late suburban sun.

Some farewells take a lifetime.

Kitchen gleaming; wife, starched and mildly tanked herself, stirring chili con carne. *I'll serve it in a tureen!* Card tables in the dining room set with tally cards and bowls of mixed nuts, ice bucket sweating on the hi-fi.

The children, talcum-powdered and sulking, build oyster-cracker forts on the Formica in protest. *It's still light outside!* But Mother finesses them with a trick from *Good Housekeeping*, a pirouette toward the table, glasses clacking on the tray that trembles above her head as she chirps, *A round of Shirley Temples for the house!*

Thursday Afternoon: Life Is Sweet

HOLLY IGLESIAS

I know what's happening, see what's coming, and try like mad to fight it. Tapioca simmers in the dented pot. *The Joy of Cooking* says to use a *bain-marie* but I say, *bain-marie, my ass*. That Rombauer woman never shopped at Goodwill a day in her life. (He'll be home in three hours.) I stir constantly, watch carefully because that's what the damned book says to do but any fool knows that the stuff is done when the spoon starts to drag.

Tapioca has many lives, grows a new skin each time a scoop's dug out. Those beady little eyes — even though the cookbook insists on calling them pearls — bounce from the box all dry and nervous and then the hot milk leaches the starch out and makes a gluey mess. The book says, *Never boil the pudding*, but screw that: I love those thick, beige swells exploding like volcanoes, the sound as the surface breaks, the smell of burnt sugar at the bottom of the pot.

They tell you, *Spoon the pudding* into individual cups, but I put the whole mess in a plastic bowl and watch it quiver as it slides into the icebox. The kids like to press little dimples into it, then lick their fingers clean behind the icebox door so I won't know who did it. Me, I push clear through to the bottom of the bowl and my finger comes out so coated that it fills my mouth.

I leave the pot on the counter, won't wash it for hours. (*Slob*, he'll say, but I'm learning to ignore him.) The residue dries into a sheet as sheer as dragonfly wings and the kids will peel it off, laughing and drooling as it melts in their mouths. I can hear them yell now as they race up the driveway, pitch their bikes against the gate. The screen door slams and in rushes the smell of them: sweat, cotton, soap, candy.

Cayenne

ANGELA JACKSON

I prepared a lamb for him (a sacrifice floating
         in herbs and
         blood and water)
         seasoned with salt of
             camouflaged tears
      onions
           and three kinds of
   peppers
        enough
        to kill
        a goat.

My mouth shaped half a plate of triumph.
I held murder in my hands.

He sat on his throne, a luxuriating storm.
His neck was stiff
as an eagle's.
He watched the sway
of my hips,
      heavy, widened
      as I walked
      with design.

He took the dish
and tasted it.
      He ground West African pepper with his teeth.
        He lulled his tongue inside the heat.
        Then
     he said, "This is not sweet enough.
          There is not enough salt."

He crushed my eyes
for salt.
He opened my veins
        for syrup
                and let my laughter over
                        lamb.
                Devoured it. (His teeth cracked bone.)
                        Devoured it. (He sucked the marrow.)

        Then
        he roared
        for more.

I gave him my mouth.
He pulled my kisses till I
was gaunt. My joints grew thin
as spider tapestries.

Still, he said he was not satisfied.

I fell behind my mask
        inscrutable
        wall of
        water
                silent hieroglyphic
                of hurt.

Reflecting,
        I watched his fine teeth
                glisten
        while he laughed.

Domestic Humiliation

ALLISON JOSEPH

What would my mother say if she could see
the piles of clothes growing larger, more frightening
in the corner of my bedroom, a bedroom that's not
really a bedroom but a living room, the bed too big
to go up the narrow stairs? What would she say

about the disarray of books and papers and magazines
that any visitor could find in piles around my bed,
yellowing scraps billowing around the floor lamps,
bank receipts, business cards, the torn envelopes
of recent correspondence, forlorn without their letters?

Would she run one accusing finger over every
bookshelf, don white gloves to shame me into dusting,
leave me coupons for furniture polish, extra-strength
pine-scented disinfectant? I want to know what
she would do, wish I was through mourning her,

so I could clearly hear her advice about reheating
leftovers, polishing tarnished silver, making gravy.
If I could get done with this grief, I'm sure I could
remember where she said to keep lettuce so it doesn't
morph into a brown rock, what she said about getting ink

out of fake silk, how she'd turn frosty chicken breasts
out of shrink-wrapped packages. If I could be less
selfish, more attentive, I could recall little details —
whether boric acid really defeats crafty roaches,
which stains get bleach, which detergent. Instead,

this apartment grows dirty in ways I didn't think
possible — dark rings in the bathtub eluding my
scrub brush, ants on the counter marching merrily
past. Until I can learn to hear what she once said,
I'll be here: grief mine, floor unwaxed, mop dry.

Kitchen

ALLISON JOSEPH

I remember this as her kitchen,
the one room in our house where no one
questioned my mother's authority —
her cast iron pots bubbling over
on the stove, cracked tea cups

in the sink. How I hated
the difficult oven always hanging
off its hinges, so loose a clothes hanger
rigged it shut, gas range whose flames
leapt beneath fingers when I turned

its knobs too quickly, floor tile
that never came clean no matter
how much dirt I swept from its
cracks. This was her domain —
kitchen for frying fish

and stewing chicken, for rice
and peas, plantains and yams,
for grease and hot sauce and seasoned salt.
Only she could make that faulty
oven door stay, only she could master

the fickle flames of the rangetop,
only she could make those worn dishes
and chipped plates fill a table
with food so rich and hot
my father could not complain.

And though I am her daughter, this house
no longer hers, her body deep in holy ground,
I know she'd want me to save all this —
decades of platters and saucers, plates,
glasses — every chipped cup, tarnished fork.

Plenty

ALLISON JOSEPH

I'm all lost in Fabric World,
the one-stop sewing supermarket
tucked in a strip mall on the
edge of town, a lonely string
of abandoned storefronts

where nothing thrives except
this lavish emporium dedicated
to needle and thread, to zippers
in all possible lengths.
Here I find patterns,

file cabinets packed with them;
I admire laces and trims,
those small decorative touches;
skim pattern catalogs complete
with color photos — all the dresses,

skirts, pants, and blouses
that anyone could sew, long as
they bought the right pattern,
right cloth. Cloth
surrounds me everywhere here,

wrapped on heavy bolts, ready
to be touched, cut. Loving
the textures I find, I walk
from aisle to aisle, whispering
fabric names: cotton, linen,

silk and wool, crepe, flannel,
fleece and gabardine, brocade,
chiffon, satin and tweed,
corduroy, denim, poplin
and seersucker. Here I find

voile, so lightweight and sheer
that I don't dare touch it;
I find velvet so lush I can't resist
letting one finger trail through
its plush nap; taffeta for airy blouses,

skimpy dresses; broadcloth tightly woven
and strong. Here are the glittery metallics
that glide off the bolt like liquid metal;
here's the fake fur, and yes, even
the double knit's here, that ill-fated

acrylic. And the designs overwhelm me:
boastful strident plaids,
tricky stripes and diagonals,
polka dots, country calico,
floral motifs, African prints.

So much for my eyes to take in —
moody midnight blues,
sensual apple reds, rich browns
the same shade as a perfectly aged
Stradivarius. Who cares that I

can't sew, that I don't have
a sewing machine to call my own,
that I have trouble seeing the eye
of almost every needle. I am here
because I love to think

of all the things that can be made
from these yards and yards of cloth,
the combinations infinite as long
as the shears are sharp, pincushions full,
threads pulled tight in every seam.

What I Learned from My Mother

JULIA KASDORF

I learned from my mother how to love
the living, to have plenty of vases on hand
in case you have to rush to the hospital
with peonies cut from the lawn, black ants
still stuck to the buds. I learned to save jars
large enough to hold fruit salad for a whole
grieving household, to cube home-canned pears
and peaches, to slice through maroon grape skins
and flick out the sexual seeds with a knife point.
I learned to attend viewings even if I didn't know
the deceased, to press the moist hands
of the living, to look in their eyes and offer
sympathy, as though I understood loss even then.
I learned that whatever we say means nothing,
what anyone will remember is that we came.
I learned to believe I had the power to ease
awful pains materially like an angel.
Like a doctor, I learned to create
from another's suffering my own usefulness, and once
you know how to do this, you can never refuse.
To every house you enter, you must offer
healing: a chocolate cake you baked yourself,
the blessing of your voice, your chaste touch.

When Our Women Go Crazy

JULIA KASDORF

When our women go crazy, they're scared there won't be
enough meat in the house. They keep asking
but how will we eat? Who will cook? Will there be enough?
Mother to daughter, it's always the same
questions. The sisters and aunts recognize symptoms:
      she thinks there's no food, same as Mommy
      before they sent her away to that place,
      and she thinks if she goes, the men will eat
      whatever they find right out of the saucepans.
When our women are sane, they can tomatoes
and simmer big pots of soup for the freezer.
They are satisfied arranging spice tins
on cupboard shelves lined with clean paper.
They save all the leftovers under tight lids
and only throw them away when they're rotten.
Their refrigerators are always immaculate and full,
which is also the case when our women are crazy.

Dinner

LAURA KASISCHKE

My mother tried to teach me how
to put a little food in each man's mouth.
She died young, and the tongue
of the mouth-harp my last father played
was steel and sharp like a knife. Now

I sit at a meal with a similar man
and we've brought what we know
about family with us
in effigy: a loaf of bread
in a lime-green bag.
I have melted the slices of dinner down
in a microwave
and set it between us. And May

has suddenly come
to our backyard. I can see
through the window beyond
the face of my husband
a cool pupa of something begun
to struggle a bit on a branch in the dusk—

The foggy dusk
turns nuclear blue
and billows the air like a dangerous cloud
and smogs up under the kitchen door
and through the cracks in the kitchen walls

like laughing gas. I dig out some more
with a plastic spoon
and my husband eats it
without speaking, just
a radio-wave that bounces
electromagnetic between us.
We have been out of butter and sugar for years

and I've never touched raw flesh
with my hands
and breakfast was always
my favorite lesson
after my mother survived the night.

In the morning I find it, hairless
and wet on the lawn. It's
the usual cocoon, though now it's gone
black as bad word spoken
over dinner

out of which no good ever comes.

Housekeeping in a Dream

LAURA KASISCHKE

The sky is a piece of mind
outside the kitchen window, the dishes
the dirt. My mother whispers
how to do it
in my ear *make a list, make*
a meal that will last
all week on Sunday, lie
to your husband, fry onions in butter until
they're soft and invisible as worms, vacuum
like it matters   so much of our flesh
is flaking away   diffusing
like pink light
through powdered milk   and wind
roars down the hallway, knocks
the houseplants to their knees.
Her photo on the wall smiles
at my broom, my back, snapped
so long ago
she isn't even ill. I nail
a cup and saucer
to the kitchen table for her:
a permanent place. She stands
outside the kitchen window, barefoot
on a crust of snow, touches
her bald white head with her fingers and cries.
I open the freezer and stare at the frost for a while, until
my face flushes white, and my neck, my hair
turns gray
and blows away
and a younger woman brings
my groceries
in brown paper bags over
the children's faces. Now
I can only see their eyes
through the holes they have scissored
to escape me. Perhaps

there was a meal
of dusk and love I should have made
but it's too late. I take a lover for something
to lie to my husband about
and forget the rest. I'm sleeping
when my family comes back.

The Visibility of Spirits

LAURA KASISCHKE

*Those ancients placed much confidence in the reality of the spirit world by
which they felt themselves surrounded. Man believed in an other-worldly
order of existence because from time to time he met its representative*

in his own world. This morning

the breeze is so fresh it's like a knife pulled
cleanly from the center
of a perfectly baked pie. The children

want pancakes for breakfast. *The skillet
is ready,* the Bisquick box says, *when*

*a few drops of water sprinkled on it
dance and disappear.* There is

a flower stuck into
a Diet Coke can on the counter. Or

maybe it's a weed. I plucked her after summer had already

set her on fire with his
blazing rages and ennui. Now

her face is orange, her eye is brown. At

the center of the brownness
there's a sound, a whispered rattle made

out of self-
pity and despair. *It isn't fair.*

Once, lying naked
beside my husband in a sweaty
bed, an awful

moth flew through an open window
and landed on my breast. It had

come from outer-space and still
had star-chalk on its face. I felt

so stunned and sure of something
I couldn't wave it away. *Hello? Hello in there I say. Who*

were you, and what happened? She looked at me
with her hairy eyes, and seemed to say, I don't

remember, and yet
I live and have
these wings for awhile, and my
girlish figure, and my
beauty queen smile, Oh

my God, I said, though I

hadn't taken the Lord's
name in vain
for a long time. And then,

Jesus Christ, Jesus Christ, Jesus Christ.

Moving Furniture

JOSIE KEARNS

I hated moving furniture.
The green couch refused to give up
its routine near the coffee table,
ruts beneath its feet deep as worry about money.
I could never remember exactly how we *did*
move it, sweating, resting a full ten minutes
after shoving the big lug, its arms and back thick
as wrestlers we saw every Saturday on TV.

Nor was shifting the stuffed rocker into
a new corner easy, like moving a bachelor
out of his apartment. But every spring
for no reason I could see, my mother moved
furniture, dusted, waxed, Pine Sol-ed,
Cloroxed, complained, wanting, I think now,
to change her life through the agency of sofas and lamps.
Like Sisyphus, she learned there are only so many
places a boulder or an end table can go.

I liked window cleaning best, the gleaming
sapphire Windex icy spray. It must be how a man
feels with the right tool for edging a lawn.
Armed with the *New! Improved!* nozzle
and twenty paper towels, I could make transparent
the world, as if everyone's seeing more clearly
depended on my ability to erase the streaks
of prism, redbluegold in the beveled glass.

The fluidity of its original firing revisited
in those glinting occlusions that bested me
every spring on those two French doors,
blonde wood stiff as Marilyn's hair.
Those tiny glass boxes were like cells in your skin
ticking, or that one month you gave up smoking.

The clarity, even in 1967 when we held
our breath: Russian spies, Brown vs.
Board of Education, Nixon's speeches.

Meanwhile, sans revolution, my mother
was moving furniture. I was cleaning the lenses
of our house to see a better world, like a geisha,
as if arranging the components
of living was enough to alter history.
It wouldn't stop my five years with a bad boyfriend,
giving up a child for adoption, or my mother's
protracting lung cancer.

But these mornings *are* our history, made of
Windex and Clorox in a rustbelt city
in the Midwest, last century. Every obstacle
in my life has been that green couch
that would not move, and especially the sun-streaked
rays of beveled French doors
currently opening for no one.

How My Mother-in-Law Instructed Me in Slaughter

SARAH KENNEDY

Brace a broomstick across the neck,
she said, and I pulled until the red head
rolled. The pullet's body sprang loose,

spraying me and the grass, and my hands
found the steaming bucket where I plunged
the carcass up and down until the feathers

loosened. Once, her arm shot past my face
when we arrived for Sunday dinner
to shove a letter at her son from his high-school

flame, but I bit my lip to blood because this
was farm life for sure, eating our own meat,
and though she slammed pans around

her kitchen and hissed, *That blue-eyed bitch,*
when the old man dropped his cane to run
for his girlfriend's daily call, she was showing me

everything I thought I needed to live
in nature. Back then, I told my friends
who went away to school and got regular

jobs that before I would give it up
for the city where my father stored
his money and my sisters, I would just die.

Maid

SARAH KENNEDY

Clorox bleaching my fingernails lady-white,
from sweet cotton swelling on the sagging line, I
would rush my father's shirts right under

the iron, sizzle them stiff with starch. Only child
allowed to touch his things, I folded perfectly
for his flight bag, my creases at his exact elbow,

my grooves at his belt-line. Even on his weekend
tractor, he'd give over good clothes only to my hand,
beckoning from the door like, I suppose you'd say,

a wife's. But he'd smile, throwing off the expensive
poplin, and for just that I would kneel to shine
his dress shoes as only I knew how, liquid sponged

around the sole, fat wax can and rag. *Either pocket,
little maid*, he'd say, patting at his pants.
Coins in one side, bills in the other. I'd always

choose the hard stuff, knowing two limp dollars
lay in the flat pleat, and when I placed the glossy
black oxfords before him, it stopped my breath

to watch quarters and dimes shimmer down,
the pennies, copper as my hair in summer,
when, oh, he would finally say I looked like him.

Ham and the Moon

JESSE LEE KERCHEVAL

Sit down
and I'll feed you.
Ladle up a bowl of lentil soup,
a little ocean
full of sun and warmth.
Add a salad made of peppers
hot as fallen stars,
avocados, olives,
a touch of lemon juice
and garlic.

I am not a world class cook
but for you, my friend,
I'll stay up all night
sweating in my kitchen
to bring the cuisine
of eleven nations
to your plate by morning.
You are sick
and you will die,
the doctors say,
but I refuse to let it be
from starvation.

So here, straight from the South,
green beans cooked all day
and my finest crabcakes,
each fork, each taste
a reason to keep living.
For dessert, cherries
so ripe they whisper
carpe diem
or would if cherries
knew much Latin.
After such a dinner,
we can wipe our mouths

clean of crumbs
and of regret.

Because I do not kid myself.
I know the future,
that iron door,
will be there waiting
no matter what
I have baking in the oven.
But in the meantime,
there are ears of sweet corn
and a mother lode of mussels
it is clear God made
especially for steaming.
Take a seat at my table.
I'll cook them up for you.

Giving the House Away

JULIE KING

The neighborhood animals are circling the yard
again. From the kitchen window, I hear
them mewling and drooling as I stir
no batter with the eggs I've forgotten to buy.

There's Leisl, Jessie's cat, and the sheltie
from next door. There's a scabbed tabby
and a ferret owned by a boy who shovels
our drive when I can't think myself into woolen
clothes. I have nothing to give them, these
animals. So I slide the air cake onto the wedding
platter, place it on the windowsill, and wait.

The animals sniff at the air, gobble it down
as if they've never eaten before,
as if they're happy. They start in on
the platter, and the sound of broken dish
scraping against esophagus worries me,
but they finish and want more. I think
to start with the registry items: the toaster,
egg cups, waffle iron. The blender, mixer,
cutting board. They gobble these, too, electric
cords on their lips, metal flakes in their fur.

The animals snuffle, their bellies full
of housewares and more hunger. How
will I tell this to my husband: no cake
on the table and no table on the floor?
The vinyl is curling up in the corners,
and I have no choice. A house is easy
to eat. Just one gentle push of the back door,
and, in no time, I could be standing naked
in my yard, the pansies blinking and blinking,
not believing their stupid little eyes.

Brick

KRISTIN KOVACIC

On her ninetieth birthday, we found her —
our tiny *Baba*, fierce, working her sponge
at the top of a thirty-foot ladder.
We squinted up her dress — our sparrow
in support hose, ancient girl without her coat,
our grandmother. *Baba, come down,*
we cried. *Baba! Before you fall!*
But there were needles in her gutters,
and the wind had left its grime, again,
on the trim of her house on the slope
on Koehler Street, America.
She shook her sooty water
on our astonishment, on our mother's iced cake
like a corpse in its pan, on Pittsburgh
far below her.

And so my father ascended
and we held the ladder fast, splinters entering
our hands like memory, another tale we'd tell
at her funeral — our crazy Croatian baba,
our Hitler of hygiene, our shelter
from the ordinary. He coaxed her down
in their language, whose first words
she'd taught him, in their soiled
country, before the war, before she placed
a coin in his immaculate palm
and did not return to claim him.

Oh Baba kids, she said, finally alighting
in her soaked slippers. *Oh Baba happy*
you come see Baba, in the loopy doll voice
my brother could imitate to make everything
sound funny. My sister helped her
find her house key, and I helped my father
destroy the ladder. I couldn't stop laughing.

You know, he said, his hatchet making stakes
of the rungs, *she loves one brick*
of this house
more than
any of you.

Covered Dish

KRISTIN KOVACIC

I wonder where it is, now.
In the dying woman's fridge, on her table,
still on the floor in her foyer, where I left it,
silent as a cat?

In her mouth?

The arrangement of each golden part.
Do I want her to see?
Do I want to create a hunger?

What she knows cannot be known. Yet here is where
I touch it: the animal — sacrificed, dissected,
washed, anointed, burnished, wrapped in silver,
delivered.

It matters not at all.
Even taken inside her, it remains
without a future; no one will ever speak of it.

She will not write a thank-you note.
Thank you for the chicken, it was delicious.
Thank you for the plums
and olives, pitted and slivered.
Thank you for rice, for almonds,
thank butter and thank onion.
Thank oil, rosemary, marjoram,
oregano, parsley, and salt.
Thank you for the cornbread, crumbs
still clinging to my fingers.

Clothesline

LAURIE KUTCHINS

Like my mother always did I hold the spare clothespins three at a time in my mouth. I
know this as silence, my mouth not a voice but a basket. She did it well,
clipped the family's clothes close and taut, maintained the line between
clean and secret dirt from wash to wash, ankles to shoulders flapping
from wire. She never understood the wind but trusted it
to whip the wash stiff and ready for the steamy hiss
of an iron under an hour of sunlight.
Silent time.

All winter the crows in the disheveled elm branches of yet another rental house haunt
the limbs above the clothesline. I do not know why they winter in these trees,
there's no food for them here, why they keep screeching above our
clothes, our dull bedding. I've adjusted to their raucous music,
their pasty droppings that turn up once in a while
like a strange berry stain in our clean, wind-
fragrant wash.

My son's clothes are getting so big yet he outgrows them faster than they wear. Soon
his favorite orange turtleneck with paint stains on the sleeves will no longer fit,
he will not be able to snap the jeans fraying in the knee where a granule
of gravel has lived a dark fleck beneath his skin since he was three.
I've given up on his socks which keep the permanent grit of
playground sand through the hearty
wash cycle.

My husband's flung shirts with their lost buttons take up so much space on the line,
sleeves that have drawn me into the smell of afternoon in his flannel shirts,
the lovely energy of his arms, the haphazard blousiness of boxers. Once
his body jolted against another line, a live wire scrambled his heart,
burned holes through his socks and workboots, killed our friend
who was then my lover. He never uses clothespins, there is
so little tidiness in his domesticity, so little
time how incredulous
he's alive.

My father's T-shirts were embarrassing and thin to me, how shapeless the worn loomed
cotton, stretched into holes the wind muscled through on the line. I don't think he
ever regretted how hard he worked through his childhood and mine, he never
named it unhappiness because he saw it as frugal necessity. He insisted
his body into its patched denims, when a sleeve was torn
it turned into a shorter sleeve, he
loved rags.

Mom took such care to dress well, she had a beautiful body, she loved to sunbathe
and sip iced coffee and read a book while waiting for the clothes to dry
on the line, she bought my older sister and me matching dresses
which meant I wore the same thing all through childhood,
the fresh and costly garment twinned with sister,
then the hand-me-down drab and
limp against my
shy skin.

Dad talked so little of his childhood, once he told me his mother Clara made ends meet
by taking in other laundry in her early widowhood. Mondays were washdays for
herself and her six children. Tuesdays through Thursdays were washdays for
money, Fridays were cleaning days, Saturdays were for cooking,
baking and bathing, Sunday was Bible school and church
and rest to get ready for Mondays to
begin again.

She kept a strict Lutheran prayer and order: youngest to oldest, Selma's dresses first,
my father's clothes next, and so on up the line. After Monday strangers' clothes
hung across the small back porch, rain or shine, the iron kept hot
on the stovetop, he once said he was always hungry, he
dreamed of a second pork chop on
his plate.

No one in that family ever speaks of Selma, her kids have not kept contact after
their mother was strangled by her new husband and stuffed into a refrigerator.
They'd met through a national Christian classifieds, Selma so happy
they found each other that way and not through looks, and fell
in love through letters and then phone calls for
a whole year before they met and
quickly married.

Spots

ESTELLA LAUTER

The cat vomits. Someone covers it with a paper towel and waits
for Mom to come home.

A husband splashes oil on his new linen shirt, a son-in-law's marinade
migrates to the beige rug. Granddaughters dribble the juice from Bing cherries
on upholstered chairs, gleefully wiping their hands on pastel shirts. One weekend
the family boat is covered with measles of sparrow shit.

This purgatory began with bright spots of blood on the old washcloths
we pinned to our underpants each month before Kotex.

The coldest water for blood, hot for fruit stains, even red wine,
which may or may not come out with salt. *Tech* for some spots, *Shout* for others,
Windex for daily kitchen grime, *Woolite* carpet potions for that partly digested cat food.
I learned to clean toilets in boarding school, where each girl took turns
at domestic work, or *dummy* we called it, even as we were being taught
to clean smart, save our souls. But five decades of expert

blotting and rubbing have produced this unforeseen conviction:
some spots, like blood, should never come out.

The Idea of Housework

DORIANNE LAUX

What good does it do anyone
to have a drawer full of clean knives,
the tines of tiny pitchforks
gleaming in plastic bins, your face
reflected eight times over
in the oval bowls of spoons?
What does it matter that the bathmat's
scrubbed free of mold, the door mat
swept clear of leaves, the screen door
picked clean of bees' wings, wasps'
dumbstruck bodies, the thoraxes
of flies and moths, high corners
broomed of spider webs, flowered
sheets folded and sealed in drawers,
blankets shaken so sleep's duff and fuzz,
dead skin flakes, lost strands of hair
flicker down on the cut grass?
Who cares if breadcrumbs collect
on the countertop, if photographs
of the ones you love go gray with dust,
if milk jugs pile up, unreturned,
on the back porch near the old dog's dish
encrusted with puppy chow?
Oh to rub the windows with vinegar,
the trees behind them revealing
their true colors. Oh the bleachy,
waxy, soapy perfume of spring.
Why should the things of this world
shine so? Tell me if you know.

Reetika Arranges My Closet

DORIANNE LAUX

Her apartment is a lesson in schematics.
The bookcase catty-corner in a corner.
Five books per shelf. No knickknacks. No dust.
On the desk a clean sheet of onionskin
fixed with a glass Bluebird-of-Happiness.
One silver pen. One wedge-of-flesh eraser.
I follow her from room to room, ooohing in awe,
windows emitting their glorious scent of Windex,
waxed floors wafting up a slick, lemony, yes.
This is the life, I quip. She sings, Tea?
and before I can answer she's opened the cupboard
to boxes stacked by size, cans in tight rows, spices
hung on the door in all their alphabetized splendor.
She leans against a sink so clean all I can think
is *inner sanctum*. She's a dark star hovering
at the window in her short jet skirt, inky V-neck
T-shirt, ebony sweater vest, sable tights, glassy black
stacked heels trussed at the instep with gold
Monte Carlo buckles. She giggles
through a sweet veil of steam rising
from the rim of her cup, her hair so black
it's blue, feathered into perfect wings.
She offers to help me organize my closet,
to separate my skirts by length and color,
throw out everything that doesn't fit,
box winter sweaters in cedar chips.
I say okay and take her to my house. We ratchet open
the front door, push past stacks of newspapers,
bags of recyclables, magazines and flowerpots —
the everything I've saved. We make our way
to the living room, stand amid its junk and rubble,
baskets and bookcases, pillows spilling
from the overstuffed couch. Photographs
and posters ascend the walls, spiny plants
fall along the sills, their tendrils looped
through narrow crevices between

the paper angels and the waterballs.
She swoons like a schoolgirl holding a ticket
for free admission to the Carlsbad Caverns,
lifts each object up from its circle of dust,
catalogs its history like an archaeologist
uncovering an ancient ruin. This, she squeals,
is great, as we high-step along the clogged hallway
to my bedroom with its four-poster strung
like a great web, the crossbars and knobs draped
with panties, socks, bras, to the closet's open doors
where she stares at the tangled spew of purses,
belts, and shoes. Reetika's oolong eyes are glowing.
Her hands are opening and closing.
I'm going to give her everything I own.

May Mowing Clover

LISA LEWIS

The art of mowing's paltry craft. I prolong
The misery of procrastination through weed
And thistle, kin to artichoke, edible if you peel
Away the spines. Two weeks and one rain suffice
To rear a bed of clover in the west back yard,
A matching patch southeast, but few dandelions
Out front: last spring's labors with a pronged tool
Paid off. By noon in May it's tricky to begin,
The heat's sinuous waves already floating
Above the street, but today I tied age-stained
Running shoes and donned shorts for the job
I still find novel, never having practiced it
Till renting a neat house in a neighborhood
Where the tune of one mower moves all residents
To shame so the whole street's a cacophony
Of buzzing blades and the air smells next to sex:
Those cut green juices flowing fresh. Priming
The mower was tough enough. I leaned close to hear
The trickle and could not: I may be deafened
In middle age, or lack right touch on rubber button,
Pressing too slow, or harsh, but finally, the gush,
And tug on cord sparked a bluish puff of oil smoke,
Staggering rumble, roar: we were off. I loved
To worry each blade to ground: is it wrong
To tear spent daffodils? Should they die back
Naturally to season next spring's blossoms?
What of wood chips ringing Bradford pear
For looks, now grown over in some species
That shears bleached at tips? Might they dull
The mower blades? Shaving the tight squeeze
Between carport posts and Toyota challenges aim
And patience, but to fail means weed-eating,
Plugging the long cord, which flops from outlet
At the slightest brush with impediment: best
To take one's chances early, and I did, with success
Due to parking closer to the wall than I dared

Last year or year before. Live and learn,
By accident: it works. I fancy the pattern
That tracks lawn's perimeter, shunting cut grass
Inwards to mow and mow again—technique
For those who own no mower bag and neither
Care to rake, as it reduces waste to finest mulch
(So I was told). Yet I've read that one must not
Repeat a pattern long for fear of forming ruts,
Or lumps; so at the center I reversed my path
And let the clippings blow across the ever-widening
Tidied spot: I would say "expanse," but it's not.
I felt bold. When blades met wood, I breasted crunch,
Squinted against splinters that flicked my shins.

The front was done in record time. I'd opened
The gate to obviate the need to prime
And start a second time, but the wind had blown it
Shut: I pried it with the mower's nose
And set in under shrubs in need of pruning.
I razored crocuses, only their striped spikes
Left from early March. I darted twixt
The plastic plugs of sewage overflow valves
And managed both to leave them whole and carve
The grass to even length. But the worst: that thick
Blossoming clover, honey waiting to happen,
White heads bobbing host to ladybugs and those
Few bees I welcome, survivors of this era's
Industrial blights and parasites: how history
Changes us, since once I feared sting's poison
And now their loss if bees attack in vengefulness.
I paced ox-like behind the laboring motor,
Slow: speed chokes the mower's undercarriage,
Wet chew in clumps. The moist stalks, decapitated,
Lay down long, did not spring up. They'd ruin
The even look I worked for, my punishment
For letting them grow—but I would feed the bees
And shirk landlords' chastisements, if only
I had the nerve. I trimmed in, edging, up, down,
Across, back, and each time watched two honeybees
Grip meaty flowers till the last. They disappeared

A minute, but by my next pass, having circled—
Squared—the lawn, they'd returned and found more
Fodder, to which they clung with hunger, tenacity,
Furred legs quivering on stalk. Through the vines
Along the fence, past the concrete turtle beneath
Which a pencil-slim snake coiled to whip away,
Exposed, and the desiccated dog turds stashed
In shaded corner near last summer's morning
Glory trellis, I forged on, and still clover rose,
Shrunken in zone, but enough for bees, that pair
I imagined twin sisters, workers, not so busy as me:
It had to happen. Either I would leave
A swatch of bee-graze or I would not. I would
Breathe courage of unconvention, know neighbors'
Glares, or bow like slashed stems and wait to rise up.
You guess how I chose. By the time I reached
That foot-wide blaze of nectared bloom, I saw
Not two bees but four, easy to count clustered
Stubborn among remains. Cowardly, I nudged
The mower across their feeding ground, and finished,
Dispatching a ladybug or two, since they fly
Sluggish. Not the honeybees. They looped up
By my face. They did not land. Then vanished
And I released the mower handle and heard
The engine die. The smell of lawn enchanted me.
Already I'd mastered my hesitation: it danced
Like a wagging bee into the sky of human pride.

Vegetable Love

DIANE LOCKWARD

My vegetable love should grow
Vaster than empires, and more slow . . .
— "To His Coy Mistress," Andrew Marvell

She bought the eggplant because her lover
had said he was leaving, and she'd read
somewhere that it was an aphrodisiac,
and she was willing to try anything,
even magic, even vegetables.

She could have bought the eggplant at the grocery store,
but because this was work that mattered,
she drove out into the country
and stopped at a roadside farm stand.
She chose the eggplant with care, the way
she might have picked out a baby or a puppy.
She found the perfect one, long, globular,
and so purple it was almost black.

One the way home, she planned how she might prepare it—
in a cold ratatouille, cubed and sautéed,
split and charcoaled over the grill,
or sliced and marinated in lime juice—
and if it worked, and she knew it would, she'd buy more.

But already it was too late. He was gone.

She remembered how it had been back
at the beginning, when he used to come home
with an armload of greens for salads,
how they would rip, shred, grate, then toss,
and feed each other, and how she had loved him.

She kept the eggplant in the refrigerator,
because although he'd said she'd grown strange,
she hoped he'd miss her and return.

It began to soften, then turned to mush.
It liquefied and leaked all over the shelves.

It grew mold and began to stink.
Each night when he did not come back,
she looked at the sodden mess, noted the changes,
told herself it was just beginning to work.

God Scrubs the Tub

God counts the rings
around the tub, numbering our baths
like the hairs of our heads. God likes
the pure grit she shakes onto her sponge.
She scours the far corner, bangs her head
on the faucet and sees stars.
The fingernails on her convincing hands
bleach white as the new moon.

God Vacuums the Pool

The carpenter bangs long nails
into the sweet wood of the deck
while God vacuums the pool in her bikini.
She is watching the tendons
of his forearms glisten in the sun.
A *good idea, muscles,* she thinks.
She sees it on the bottom then,
wonders if it's *playing* possum.
In her infinite wisdom, knows better.
As with all death, better gone than going,
she thinks. God knows had she arrived earlier,
seen him circling, she'd have been bound
to save him. She sighs. Even now
the dead can't rise without her help.

God Packs Lunches

God spins the peanut butter thin
as silk onto the dense bread, covers
each pore so the Smucker's red
can't penetrate. When she comes to the end
of the loaf she turns the last piece facing
in. You won't even notice it's a heel.

Lemons

GAIL MARTIN

Today the bass booming
through the neighborhood is sad,
like the nuisance rose that comes back wilder

with each harsh pruning. One day
I will rip it out altogether, wearing leather gloves
to the elbow. I want to cry at all of it: the energy

of the newlyweds next door, their confidence
tackling lawn grubs, the zeal of their decorating, their fights.
How shiny black their grill. And the German shepherd

pup, ears and nose too long for who he is today,
and the bravado of the girl spray-painting
her flip-flops gold for the prom, the knees

of the mailman, still white in April, exposed
below the regulation bermudas.
I am not talking remembrances here, nor ruin.

This is not the loneliness of my grandmother's elephant
brooch, red, white and blue rhinestones resting in my jewelry box, not
the cousin who ate candles the last three days he was alive.

It is not even a longing for the reliable fathers
in the old neighborhood, that insistent piano note
backed by strings. Today I tear up seeing vinegar

and oil refuse to mix, watching the bastard
across the street repaint the little Amish buggy
and figurines and set them for summer

on his unused porch, his tulips lined up singly,
sousaphone players in a high school band.
Today the lawnmower starts and the newspaper slaps

the front door. I see the pantry shelves crowded
with canned soup and peaches, how
lemons stacked in a white bowl resemble grief.

What Lies Beneath

SHARA MC CALLUM

The woman inside turns flour to dumplings
with the magic of water and salt.
Her hands move without thought.

Outside her window, girls gather,
whispering secrets in corners,
laughing at jokes she can't hear.

She is their age again, home in Trinidad —
swimming out to a nearby dock and falling
asleep in the afternoon sun. Night:

and the shore retreats from her reach;
the water fills with shadows. She hears
her father calling from land's edge.

Why doesn't she answer? Why is she afraid
with his voice instructing her path home?
She has forgotten this story a long time now.

Chopping carrots, her hands become the flashing knife.
Fingers dashing from bag to board, she pauses
to brush a loose hair from her eyes,

trying not to see herself shivering
in the cooling air, the sea beneath her
kept at bay by a few pieces of wood.

Home Remedy

PAULA MC LAIN

I smoothed and blocked my hands like a shirt in a gift box.
Snow fell, soiled. Ice released the house.
My son began to walk — I know this now —
but everything came to me through water. His cry
was a bubble breaking just past me.

I slumped to the floor in the pantry,
head resting on a bag of heat-softened vidalias,
but then there were baseboards to consider,
and the industry of black ants in my white rice.
I got up.

It took me half a day to walk to the refrigerator,
but once I was there I knew why.
I faced the labels of the mustard, the marmalade,
the baby gherkins. I filled the ice trays,
set a flank steak out to thaw.

In this way the days pass: the TV speaks to the spin cycle.
I can make the dishes last three hours, passing my index nail
inside the tines and over the knotted flowers
on the flat of each fork. *Trillium*, I want to say,
but they could be footprints,

some tiny thing letting me know it's been here all along.

Third Stair, Seventh Stair, Landing

JANE MEAD

I

Later, the doctor called Shiva Kincaid will send me home saying "Double
your anti-depressants and suck on a lemon," but for now I lie a little, and
polish the stairs: when Linda asks what stair I'm on, third I say, or seventh —
because really they are always the stairs to elsewhere, aren't they, and those
the sacred numbers, meaning wholeness, perfection, balance, and such.

And then there's my version of hands to work, heart to god, — housework
done in silence: I have begun more poems while washing dishes than I
can say, found the thought by surprise as I sweep, solved the problem while
changing sheets. It's a version of what Einstein called the three B's, the three
places where life makes room for inspiration — bus, bath and bed. I think it
was Einstein, I think we all know what he meant. This is housework done
in silence; this is no husband, no children. I have no idea how artists with
children do it — but I bow a little now in their direction.

Sometime in the third hour of our phone call, Linda says "I've made lentil
soup while we've been talking." She gives me the recipe — it's simple and
wholesome, and she says she hopes I'll try it, — and I say I will, but I know I
won't — I hate cooking and so I don't cook. No husband, no children. Then
she asks again what stair: fifth, I say, no, — seventh, though really I'm folding
laundry — shoulder pressing the phone to my jaw, where later the pea-size
lump will develop — the one that requires the lemon.

II

My mother lives on a pecan farm in a 30' x 30' house — a house, half adobe,
half frame, which was built long ago for migrant farm workers in the town
of Rincon, on the Rio Grande, far south in New Mexico. Not long ago she
added on the largest private sunroom in the western hemisphere, because she
is in her 70s, has had cancer, and gets sinus infections if there is so much as a
cool breeze in the next county — which there often is. In the sunroom there is
a grand piano, a portrait of her mother (now 96) as a small girl, a velvet sofa,
a coffee table that belonged to her grandmother, and several potted lemon
trees. Mostly it's a huge expanse of Saltillo tiles, with an adobe wall to the
windy side, and row of windows and French doors on the other.

My mother is of puritan stock — a WASP — who packed up her three children and moved from Boston to New Mexico when she was in her forties and recently divorced — moved to New Mexico because she remembered going through on the train as a child, remembered what was to her an utterly foreign kind of beauty. She took up farming in her 50s. She travels to Europe once every couple of years to see friends, but is otherwise frugal by nature and upbringing: she saves envelopes, washes plastic bags, eats the rotten fruit first. She has a stovetop, a toaster oven, and an outside grill. It has never occurred to her to install an oven, though she is an accomplished cook, and she wouldn't dream of buying a microwave. Junk. The only heat comes from some contraption in the bathroom — which is the same size as the other three rooms — the house is split into four rooms of equal size. It is spare and beautiful — to me it has always looked like a work of art. I don't believe she owns anything ugly. The silverware is a complete mishmash — we learned our family tree by squinting at the initials. She can make a pair of Levis last longer than anyone I know, and her farm truck is a real junker — I have never driven a truck with gears that were harder to shift.

III

My friend Maryanne and I are out picking up pecans in the orchard. It is a cold windy day — which in southern New Mexico means very windy, lots of grit. My mother has had a mastectomy perhaps as little as a week earlier — I am still draining the wound for her in the mornings and evenings. But there she goes by in the junker, a sight to behold — the neighbor's dog on the roof of the cab, braced and skidding, — barking herself into a frenzy, my mother's dog riding shotgun, and the truck sounding like something out of the stock car races. My mother is so bundled up against the cold that she looks like a cartoon character — and as the whole noisy mess of them goes by, Maryanne looks at me and says "That's your mother." "I know," I say and we laugh.

Inside, in the kitchen the size of the bathroom, the neighbor's girl Margaret is ironing the linen dish towels. I do not know her.

Some women marry houses

SARAH MESSER

I

My mother, blind from the swamp-gas,
the kudzu, almost married
a gas-station — had five or six
kids in a cardboard box backyard;
almost drank motor-oil in a styro-
foam cup; almost slept
with the drawer to the register open
under ghost Esso, flies licking
lip-corners, a wide-wale
corduroy grin; almost burned
our infant skin off, birthing on those
gas-rags —
                           But this
did not happen. She married
a meat-shop owned by a prominent
butcher. He puts a neat bullet
in the temple of every yearling.
*It's painless, they don't even know
how they die.* Each evening she takes
buckets outside and washes
the red walls down.

II

Each day, my grandmother walked
a bridge of stretched cat intestines
under horsehair power lines.

Her husband found her often inside
the belly of a violin. She was all
he ever wanted in a woman: exotic as
the parlor's Oriental, the throats
of his seven caged birds. He steamed
stripped wood and clamped it
to her body. He glued seams

and clefts above the sacral
joints he kneaded each night when
they made love, so she could sing
all those pretty high notes
from inside their polished home.

III
I live alone and love
the abandoned walls, the water-
damage, the shelf-paper
tongues lolling from cabinets, mid-morning
sunlight on telephone wires, the telephone,
the leafy, leaning second-story porch.

It's easy to love the house, so quiet
in the haze of morning windows —
it's easy to love the chimney, still warm
from last night's fire, and solid
at the center, something to put my hands upon
when no one will enter me.

Convolvulus Tricolor

LESLIE ADRIENNE MILLER

for Jutta and Corinne

Two women. Easy together in the twilight, and I
third, but taken in like the skittish coonhound,
his doggy capacity for adoration broken

before he came to them. *Six months,* Jutta says,
before his tail went up again. They show me
photographs — the garden before they wrested it

from the mountain's wish to be stony, the dog
younger, the two of them with longer hair,
their *motos,* meals, a tent on a beach. Three

of us now in the beans pulling green cords, filling
a white bowl. Corinne pulls an aloe open, presses
the gum to her wrists, mine. Jutta hands a wand

of zucchini over the wall, comic, shorn of the flower,
long as a horse's prick, all the words for this in French,
German, English. Green, striped, soft skinned. Corinne

will slice it into flat rounds, dollops of sour cream, nests
of cheese. Jutta will lift white cakes of fish into butter,
trim a clove of garlic above the pan. Bean steam.

Bluing of evening. Corinne bends inside a vine, skull-sized
leaves of the zucchini sneaking off into the woods, snips
near each bud so the flowers don't tap out the vine's desire

to bear fruit. The dill already yellow, September a step
away, breath of the river cooling the terraces, sage pouring
ears over the path. Corinne stands up, says soon it will be

wood we're cutting. Hunches back into the vine. I leaf
through the stacks of photos, hungry for their former
joy: one of them on a curve, a gorge angling away,

bright plats of snowshoes in a pile, splayed
yellow chicken beside a knife. The other naked,
asleep on a blanket beside the Red Sea. Helmets

stacked by a road, lichen, mist. Both of them
on a good morning, tousle-headed, sleepy-eyed
with the pleasure of that time. I pour them each

a glass of wine — want the endless meal of their intimacy
to stay in the frame. What they are is what I remember
seeing through windows at twilight in another country:

more precisely, Baltimore, peering into the yellow squares
of the lowest windows along Charles Street with my then
lover, having something. Not enough. In every window

a life more resonant than ours, heads bowed to meals,
a steaming pot, her feet across his knees, dishes
plunged against a porcelain sink, quiet murmur from

another room, *come now,* one ruby lozenge of wine
left rocking toward stillness in the glass on the sill.
Even broken, their past is a place I want to go again,

complicitous with what they remember, *yes more
photos,* I say, before they divvy them up like cash.
Our worst fears are small enough to travel in pockets,

the brutality of simple purpose. The zinnias now too tall
for their leggy stalks, fall against the path, weighted
with their own drifting heads. Corinne's eyebrows

like birds' wings fly up. She's asking me again
if it's true I don't believe in love that lasts,
that question that loosens a little ting of pain, fork

against a glass, but it wasn't me she was asking.
We've traded all our hope for knowledge, then wanted
back our lavish faith. *Hundreds of years ago,* she says,

these terraces were home to grapefruit trees. It's plain
as bread, the strict economy of women. No one of us
has spoken nor need speak of mothers: what they were

was breath, leverage, space, and what the world was,
was itch, necessity, but not an industry. We are
momentarily water in the twilight, seeping, feeding,

beneath the work of time. The purple blossoms
are only open until eleven in the morning.
Come before then, Jutta says, *and you will see all.*

The Days of My Mother

LAUREL MILLS

Today is washday. My mother
hooks the old tub to faucets
over the slate sink, wrestles cotton sheets
through wringers, hangs them outside
on the sagging clothesline.
Tuesdays she irons, setting up
the heavy board with its scorched pad,
dampening our blouses and skirts
with a Coke-bottle sprinkler,
testing the iron's heat with her finger.
We wait for the middle of the week,
when she wears a flour-smudged apron
to fill date cookies, stir *Kiss* pudding,
shake warm doughnuts in a bag of sugar
to feed our impatient hunger.
Thursdays she claims as her own,
translates Latin essays, scours
Reader's Digest Condensed Books,
crafts poems on backs of grocery slips,
weeds her flowers and studies birds.
On Fridays, she cleans for the weekend,
scrubbing the kitchen linoleum on her knees,
pushing the tired Electrolux over the carpet,
shaking fresh-smelling sheets onto the beds,
waxing the piano my sisters play.
Most days, my mother nearly forgets
the life she'd once intended for herself.

At Thirty

KYOKO MORI

for my mother

September: six months into the last full
decade of your life. I am learning to

spin. In my right hand, I hold the wool
lightly, careful not to squeeze, tug with

the left, and watch the thread spin out like
a life line as the drop spindle glides

down. The summer's with us still. Every morning,
the gladioli I bring into the house are tall

dolls in ruffled costumes — salmon, purple, dark
red. Saturday afternoon, a black

bee drowses on a white shirt on the line,
an inch or so above the heart. At my

friend's house, we've frozen one hundred green peppers,
halved and washed, each wrapped in plastic like a child's

gift. Picking cherry tomatoes and cucumbers, their
blossoms like fiery bells, I remember

your garden, your salvias and celosias
jewel-red into early fall. Sunny

afternoons, as I drive to work, the sky
explodes with yellow maples. Not many have

begun to shed. The roadside is blurry with
aster, chicory, their soft blue light. I

wish I could stop the time now, the season
and my life in perfect balance, a dizzy

suspense.

Bread

SHARON OLDS

When my daughter makes bread, a cloud of flour
hangs in the air like pollen. She sifts and
sifts again, the salt and sugar
close as the grain of her skin. She heats the
water to body temperature
with the sausage lard, fragrant as her scalp
the day before hair-wash, and works them together on a
floured board. Her broad palms
bend the paste toward her and the heel of her hand
presses it away, until the dough
begins to snap, glossy and elastic as the
torso bending over it,
this ten-year-old girl, random specks of
yeast in her flesh beginning to heat,
her volume doubling every month now, but still
raw and hard. She slaps the dough and it
crackles under her palm, sleek and
ferocious and still leashed, like her body, no
breasts rising like bubbles of air toward the
surface of the loaf. She greases the pan, she is
shaped, glazed, and at any moment goes
into the oven, to turn to that porous
warm substance, and then under the
knife to be sliced for the having, the tasting, and the
giving of life.

the shekhinah as mute

ALICIA SUSKIN OSTRIKER

our mothers tremble vibrate
hesitate at the edge of speech
as at an unmade bed, their mouths work, confused

our mothers helpless to tell us
She whom you seek sacrificed
her place before the throne

divided into the atomic structure
of matter and hides there
hair wings streaming

womb compassionate pitiless
eyes seeing to the ends of the universe
in which life struggles and delights in life

they cannot take our hands show us
how to take comfort in raisins and apples
break apart laughing spit seed

they cannot say *seek me*
they teach us cooking clothing craftiness
they tell us their own stories of power and shame

and even if it is she who speaks through their mouths
and has crawled through ten thousand wombs until this day
we cannot listen

their words fall like spilled face powder

Grief Comes in Smallest Ways

GAILMARIE PAHMEIER

For the first time in months
she's making meat loaf.
He imagines the casual manner
in which she cracks an egg,
the way it slides down the sides
of the glass bowl to marry
beef, yellow onion, bell pepper, spice.
He imagines it is abandon
that pulls her hands
into the bowl;
he imagines it is delight
that carries her as egg soaks
into meat between her fingers.
He wishes she would wear
a short full apron,
someplace to leave the stick
she rubs from her palms.
He wishes she'd always bake meatloaf.

She works out, sweats.
She shows him often
how her arms are strong,
that with her legs
she can lift a weight
he'd have died
to save her from.
She calls from the kitchen.
He finds her sitting,
legs scissored open.
Look, she says,
and brings her chest
to rest against the floor.
You're lovely, he says.
I like the way your skin looks

pulled tight against your thigh.
I like the way the kitchen light
moves brilliant through your hair.
I like the way things smell.

Sunday Baking

GAILMARIE PAHMEIER

for Miller Williams

He thinks she cannot see him through the window,
smoking his cigar in the slow Sunday dusk.
That's what these evenings are for,
smoking and reading an easy magazine.
From a chair on the porch he moves to watch her,
kneading and pulling this day's bread.
He should speak, offer his assistance.
He could grease the pans and sweep the flour dust,
pull the damp hair away from her forehead
as she smiles and stretches this thing she knows.
But the kitchen seems crowded when she works,
full of the several people she has been.
The girl whose cupped hands splashed his back,
the one whose fingers learned his skin,
the woman whose whole body is in this baking.
It is the hands of this woman that haunt him.
Although it is a damn thing, it carries him.
The bread's in the oven, and the smell
of love is thick inside, and he knows
that the bread, the woman, and the house are not his,
that this is what is meant by home.

The Soup

PEGGY PENN

On the day of your scan, I make a soup
to wean us from meat. Beans soak and blanch
an hour while I slit open the cell-
ophane wrap on the celery, chopping
the ribs into small pieces, the size
of the stones that follow an avalanche.
Carrots sliced into see-through orange mem-
branes, others hacked into jagged boulders, bi-
sected as though by the pressure of shift-
ing plates. Onions at knife point suppurate
and toss themselves into the hot oil. What
is left? two blind see-no-evil potatoes.
Sweet herbs: I pull apart ovate leaves
of basil and sweet marjoram. Red kidney
beans slip out of their bladder skins, rubbing
against the Great Limas. Together,
they give off a kind of scum which keeps down
the foaming boil; instead it heaves and
swells, trembling like a bosom but does not
spill out. Thank God for scum! *I rinse my knife*,
watching its gleaming edge rotate under
the water; now there is only the wait.

Cooking Lesson

ZARINA MULLAN PLATH

My mother is casual when I ask
for her secrets: how to make *gulab
jamun*, or meaty *pulao*, or sweet brown
Parsi rice with its sharp angles of cinnamon
stick and clove. She shrugs over the heaping
plates at India Garden, pops another fold
of warm *naan* into her mouth and lets
the waiter refill her glass.

Bisquick, she says, for the *gulab
jamun*. Powdered milk and sugar syrup.
She is more guarded about the rice — offers
no details about the chopping and frying,
gives no clue to her careful method
of baking the pot just so long — changing
the subject between forkfuls of vegetable
korma and coconut chutney.

I've come to know this silence, this easy
dismissal when I ask about the hazy image
in an old photo, or the closed-door
mutterings of my aunts. My mother's
stories are sifted away in her canisters
and jars, history doled out sparingly
with turmeric. I can only lean into her
at the stove, watch her massage saffron
into her bubbling kettle, and guess
at what she knows when
she raises the hot spoon to her lips.

All the Soups

MARTHA RHODES

All the soups I've made in my life —
slow-cooking easy broths, red thick
puréed blends. Churning it all up
alone in my kitchen, tasting,
covering, uncovering, remembering
spat-out carrots pinched between Mother's fingers
and pressed back into my mouth, Mother
wanting to get done with those meals, running
upstairs before Father comes home, Father
grubbing through drawers looking for pints,
both sisters up in the field getting plastered
and laid, me stuck in that chair,
locked behind a metal tray, not knowing
who's slamming the screen door so hard
that waves in my milk cup spill to my lap.
There's always a pot of soup on the stove.
I trace cats and houses on the damp kitchen wall,
waiting for anyone to come home,
waiting for one person
hungry enough to come home.

Song of the Cook

NATASHA SAJÉ

I chant the pickled alewife, I wallow in surfeit

    plums simmering magenta
    culled & staining
    a backdrop for intrigue

    I excise hearts

I let edges be edges and
where would I be without my thin blade?

Somewhere a woman is washing her hands with wine
on her breath, and elsewhere garlic
heads tumble to a pink tiled floor

My fingers are forks, my tongue is a rose

    herb-snip
    meat-whack
    root-chop

I turn silver spoons into rabbit stew
make quinces my thorny upholstery

O custard apple pudding of applied love
O cider wheedling its sugary tune

how else could the side of beef walk
with the sea urchin roe?

How else could I seize what I see and ride
my bird's-eye maple broom

    into the night sky's steam?

What I Want to Make for You

NATASHA SAJÉ

First I'll find two pears,
green speckled with yellow,
the color of locust trees in May,
two specimens that yield
to slight pressure from my thumb.
They'll sit in the sun, next to an apple
whose ethylene breath will ripen them more,
to the point where even the faintest touch
would bruise them. Then I'll spread out
several leaves of phyllo, sweet
buttering each one with a sable brush,
between whose sheets I'll slip
toasted, slivered, blanched almonds.
I'll cut the pastry into hearts,
one for each of us, baking until crisp —
not long — in the hot oven waiting.
You haven't forgotten the pears?
My knife is so sharp it won't hurt
when I peel and slice them.
More sweet butter and sugar sizzle
in a pan, plus heavy cream,
unctuous, languid, sleepy,
and the pears with some eau de vie,
then a rapid simmer.
Now the assemblage:
One nutty heart on the bottom,
soft sautéed pears in the middle,
another fragile heart on top.
A pool of glossy caramel cream,
also on my fingers with which I offer you
ce mille feuille croquant de poire
au caramel.

Duties and Vocations

JANE SATTERFIELD

Ashes to ashes, dust to dust—
Dust-rhinos lurk beneath the bed.
I hate to clean but clean I must.

I have no servants unimpressed
By anything I write or read.
Ashes to ashes, dust to dust—

My house is closing in, disas-
ter I cannot escape. Misled,
I hate to clean but clean I must,

Scrubbing the filthy pipe whose rust
Clings to cast-iron pipes of lead.
Ashes to ashes. Dust to dust.

By housework am I cruelly blessed—
Is it eccentric to have said
"I hate to clean but clean I must,"

when housework fills me with disgust?
What fulfills me most lies ahead.
Ashes to ashes, dust to dust.
I hate to clean but clean I must.

Wintering

JANE SATTERFIELD

for Ned Balbo

The worst winter in ages — pipes freeze, nerves fizzle,
tempers flare then even more descends
as one more snowfall starts, a swirl of flakes

over laden boughs, what is already
perilous . . . The slushy ruts thaw, refreeze,
and once again the work of digging out

as the urban flat takes on the isolation
of the moors. Still one lost soul
will brave it, drop round for a drink and so the story

detonates — what lies ahead (the branches out),
the ground below (sterile, demythologized),
the hidden flame at the heart of the house

and the slight girl who slips out, well aware
the lock is turned behind her. Hears the elevator's
tension cables, just that clattering there.

Furious Cooking

MAUREEN SEATON

for Susan and Vanessa

It's the kind of cooking where before you begin
you dump the old beef stew down the toilet

and flush it thinking, good, watching
gravy splatter on the shiny white tiles.

Where the chicken spread-eagled on the butcher block
could be anyone and you don't even bother to say

thanks for your life, chicken, or regret the way
the little legs remind you of just that.

Where the bay leaves aren't eased in but thrown
voilà into sizzling olive oil which

burns the *poulet* nicely along with the onions
alerting the fire alarm and still you think,

good, let the landlord worry I'll burn this bitch down.
It's that kind of cooking that gives your family

agita, big Italian-style pain, even if it's only
fricassee the way your Nana used to make it.

She was so pissed she painted her kitchen ceiling red!
Remember the Irish soda-bread chicken and all those

green veggies in heavy cream your poor mother
yelled so loud about, oh, the calories! Furious

cooking, the kind where hacking the *pollo*
to bits with no names, you look up to see the windows

steamed like a hothouse. In fact, it's so hot
you strip to bare skin and now you're cooking mad

and naked in just that bartender's smock with the screw
you'd like to stick into some big cork right now.

Cooking everyone can smell from the street. What
the fuck, they say, and hurry home to safe food, yours

a rank hit of ablution and sacrifice, although
no one recognizes the danger. I used to wonder

about the Portuguese woman on the first floor,
what that odor was that drifted up on Saturdays

into my own savory kitchen. How it permeated
Sunday and Monday as well, all that lethal food left

to boil on her big stove from the old country.
Now I know she was just furious cooking, that aroma was

no recipe you'd find in any country, a cross between
organs and feathers and spinal fluid and two eyes,

not to mention the last song in that chicken's throat
before it kicked the bucket in the snow in the prime

of life when all it ever wanted you could etch on a dime
and spin blithely into a crack in the kitchen table.

In the Kitchen Dancing to Kitty Wells

HEATHER SELLERS

The blinds are up, the dusty screen breezing.
It's 9 P.M. and the kids are playing Starcraft online,
Hovering over the computer terminal, stuck to the vinyl.
It's September and still summer and still hot and still.
We are in love in a kind of jagged way, I don't always
Love this dishes undone life. I'm still dreaming.

This we know. You ask about my time. I pull you into
My arms. You are the better dancer from the waist up,
I'm superior from the hips to the floor, we jab and jibe
And then you put on the music. And the moon comes over
The steel sink. And the dirty dishes look bohemian and cool.
And the kids come in to see why. And you
Open another bottle of cheap Foxhorn chardonnay, which
We have convinced ourselves is golden good. I am barefoot.
You are never barefoot. The boys pull out my hair clips.
I ask them to dance (I ask them to vacuum I ask them to fold),
I motion with my arms, dance monster.
All that girl smothering, all that the boys settle into their
Boxes of light, and me and the dad into our boxes and balances.
Moon glow, television glow, Starcraft glow — we're lifted up
Into the song of night, like any little dancing vague family.

One Quick Quiz

PAULA SERGI

Would this help: a grocery list with color codes
assigned to aisles with the four basic food groups —
no more running back for bread or milk? Can you pay
an overdue at the video store with credit or debit?
And how does one decide between the two?
She has lost another discount card under

the wire wheels of the market's cart
or maybe under bills on the dining room table
under the soccer schedule,
under dog-eared magazines that offer
to locate her personality with one quick quiz,
just after the article on ways to save

her marriage. And if she opens the hamper
will a tepid sludge of laundry spill out,
a cache of forgotten clothes, mismatched
socks, pants whose waists have gone limp,
shirts whose wrists have frayed, unwashed and loaded
with that stored-too-long smell, dank and now

permanently trapped in the fabric's very fibers?
She has misplaced her children's faces,
the dumb infant stares, elementary grins, high school
sheen and glamour, uncatalogued in a shoe box
under dust, under an unsuspecting sofa, green
under floral under plaid as the styles change, reupholstered,

rearranged to make do like her hair under spray,
under mousse under perm under rinse and highlights
to camouflage the grey, which even now in the perfumed
air of the salon, after all this time under the dryer
can be seen underneath, detected

like the hairdresser's bored, vacant smile,
real interest hidden or erased like wisps of hair
under tape in the yellowed baby book,
under the rocker and the four post bed,
under the swiveling stylist's chair.

Purpose

DIANE SEUSS

I think all day about how terrible
it would be to drop it by accident
until at the end of the day (it's been
a difficult day) I break it on purpose

and then quickly vacuum it up and feed
the dogs and carry up a load of wash
(I believe it's the fifth load though it could
be the fourth load) and spread my red velvet

pants out on the dining room table to dry
as the label says *Hand Wash* and I didn't
hand wash, I washed them in the machine
set to *Delicate.* That's a lie, I've never

changed the washer setting dial in my whole
life but if I put them in the dryer I knew they'd
shrink and I can't afford to lose
another pair of pants.

And then the dog leaped up
and got the donut out of the bag, the dog leaped
up, leaped higher than I've ever seen a dog
leap, truly, the dog . . . well, it was impressive

is what I'm saying. He ate the donut, carried
it off under my bed and ate it, and I remembered
my dream last night, I couldn't find my purse
and I was bleeding from between my legs

and when I finally did find my purse (after
a scene with a roomful of bats and flying squirrels)
I looked at it, my suede purse (I don't have
a suede purse) and it was on fire, I had to

stop the car and extinguish the burning purse
with snow. I looked "purse" up in the dream
dictionary later and it said "vagina." I looked
up "purse" and it said, "self, identity, vagina."

Flying squirrels were not in the dream dictionary.
Menstrual blood was not in the dream dictionary.
I'd been cleaning all day. There was a feeling
that something was coming to a close. Like I was

preparing the house for something. So much
wash, up and down the stairs, every time I think
how much it would hurt to fall carrying
the laundry basket. Now it's down to two really

tall piles of wash, a black pile and a white pile.
And in the dream insects were going at my bare
feet. Then I wrote a letter, revealing everything
to the recipient. I mean I told the whole story.

I said everything there was to say on the subject.
I remember when I was nursing my baby, it was
three or four in the morning and the room was
dark except for moonlight coming in the window.

I thought, "there are millions of women all over
the world doing this same thing this very moment"
and it made me dizzy thinking of it, and now
the same thought occurs to me, there are millions

of people all over the world doing this thing
that I'm doing, moving their fingers in this particular
way, thinking these thoughts even, maybe they
accidentally splashed bleach on the black clothes,

maybe their dog ate the donut, maybe they'd never
before turned the dial to *Delicate*, maybe they revealed
everything, maybe they worried about breaking
it, but did anyone else in the world break it on purpose?

Entropy

FAITH SHEARIN

My mother's kitchen was asleep.
Our family didn't gather there:
we lived and ate in our bedrooms
hypnotized by the blue lights of TV.
But, in her kitchen, pots and pans
floated, belly up, in the week-old
water, and our garbage, smiling,
outgrew its bag. All of this very

slowly, as if in a dream. My mother
despises what can never truly
be done so she does not care for cooking
or cleaning. If one cooks a fine dinner
one must wash the dishes to cook
a fine breakfast to wash the dishes
to cook a fine lunch and so on. My mother
explained this one afternoon in the basement
where the laundry grew around us like trees.

Our jungle-home was a metaphor for
my mother giving in to entropy.
When wine spilled on the couch and we
laughed as the stain unfurled,
we were embracing chaos. When we
fell asleep with the lights on
and the TV talking, we were
the weeds in our own garden.

My mother's kitchen was haunted.
Her refrigerator leaned to one
side and made only brown ice.
Her biscuits were as flat as plates.
But none of this mattered because
we were forgetting ourselves
even as we were becoming ourselves.

We pursued truth, beauty,
the meaning of life while

my mother's kitchen discovered
decay. All this unraveling —
moldy food, newspapers
piling up to the ceiling.
We loved each other like that:
bananas going black on the counter,
lines coming in around our eyes.

The Sinking

FAITH SHEARIN

I am bent over a sink of heavenly suds
    my hands moving like angels in wind

when I find myself weepy with work I will never
    make done. Beside me a garbage bag opens

and fills like some hungry lung and my newest shoes
    wear the fine lines of age. Even as I gaze

at the just-folded laundry I am seeing the first shirt
    I will open the way a diver opens water.

As a child I wondered at my mother's lost days
    in the polite lines of banks and supermarkets:

her head bowed as if in grief. Later I read we each lose
    years looking for lost objects and waiting for red lights

to change. One third of our earthly time passes on in our sleep.
    After one bill is paid another moves close like an enemy.

It's no wonder cavemen left only their own bones
    and a few reddened sketches of the hunt. My life story

is a series of telephone bills paid too slowly and dental visits
    for cavities I can't feel. Have I mentioned the car tags

I lost in the couch while kissing? They seem such a waste —
    these days I barely remember — doing the work that has no

meaning, the work that will whirl on above me when my body
    has crossed its arms to everything

and dirt loosens and falls into my heart like rain.

Immaculate Lives

CATHY SONG

We long for the quiet
domesticity of those Dutch interiors,
the girl at the window,
head bent over a piece of sewing
so that the light
saturating the deft plaits
would take our breath away.
They were right.
In praise of light,
they gave us hair,
the honey yellows,
terrains of ochre, mustard, amber
to offset the rational tiles,
the black-and-white squares,
laid as if for a game of chess,
the courtly pattern in which they moved,
restrained, knowing the intricate rules.
A flood of letters never cluttered the table.
A pitcher of milk, a simple meal
could trigger a sumptuous
feast of architecture and light.
They savored what they knew,
intelligence and discipline
bearing fruit in domestic discovery —
the mirror a velvet lake.
If they chose to speak,
they did so expensively,
each word the weight of gold
coins in exchange for silence.
The heavy clink of meaning.
We could learn such thrift.
A flurry of papers like insects swarm our doorsteps.
We waste a thousand words
and still have not said it,
or said it a thousand times.
They have cleaned their houses for us,

swept and tidied the kitchen,
hid the pail of slop from view.
We move like pawns toward checkmate —
the pristine corner
chiseled by the diamond light
and the dazzling dexterity of our hosts,
the lacemaker, the glassblower —
stunned at the immaculate lives
we are unable to keep.

A Poet in the House

CATHY SONG

Emily's job was to think.
She was the only one of us
who had that to do.
—Lavinia Dickinson

Seemingly small her work,
minute to the point of invisibility —
she vanished daily into paper, famished,
hungry for her next encounter —
but she opened with a string of humble
words necessity,
necessary as the humble work
of bringing well to water, roast to knife, cake to frost,
the coarse, loud, grunting labor of the rest of us
who complained not at all
for the noises she heard
we deemed divine, if
claustrophobic and esoteric —
and contented ourselves to the apparent,
the menial, set our heads
to the task of daily maintenance,
the simple order at the kitchen table,
while she struggled with a different thing —
the pressure seized upon her mind —
we could ourselves not bear such strain
and, in gratitude, heaved the bucket,
squeezed the rag, breathed the sweet,
homely odor of soap.
Lifting dirt from the floor
I swear
we could hear her thinking.

The Sky-Blue Dress

CATHY SONG

The light says *hurry* and the woman
gathers the perishables to the table, the fish
thawed to a chilled translucency, the roses
lifted out of a sink of rainwater, the clean hunger
on the faces of her husband and her children faithful
as the biscuits they crumble into their mouths.
Hunger is the wedge that keeps them intact,
a star spilling from the fruit
she slices in a dizzying multiplication of hands
wiping a child's mouth of butter, hands
wiping a dishrag across a clean plate.
She stands at the door waving the dishrag—
ready, set, go!—calling the children in, shooing
the children out, caught in a perpetual
dismantling, a restlessness she strikes the rag at
as if she could hush the air invented by flies.

The light says *hurry* and the family
gathers at the table, the tablecloth washed through countless
fumblings of grace, its garland hem of fruits clouds
into blue pools, faded as a bruise or a reckless tattoo or the roses
the woman hurried that morning into the house,
rushing to revive the steaming petals out of wet
bundles of newspaper the roses traveled in
up the mountain from the market by the sea,
flowers more precious than fish
she left spoiling in the backseat of the car.
Petals and flesh are perishable as the starfruit
a friend of the family climbed the tree to save,
tossing to earth what the sun, the birds, the insects
were days, hours, minutes from rotting.
The roses, stems cut at a slant under rainwater,
breathe cool nights into the air thick with biscuits.
On the table beside the roses a dish of butter disappears
as each knife swipes
its portion, its brightness, its wedge of cadmium lemon.

The light says *hurry* and the man
begins to paint roses while his wife tosses in her sleep
and dreams of a dress she wore long before
she was married, a dress that flowed to her feet
when her hair swirled at her knees, swirled
even when she was simply standing under a tree.
The man who was just a boy then remembers
the first time he saw her, she was standing in a river of hair,
remembers this as he begins to paint roses.
She dreams of the sky-blue dress,
how she once filled it with nothing but skin.
Flesh does not fill it.
Neither does wind.
The girl who wore it left it
pinned like a hole in the sky
the woman passes through, sleep
pouring out of her into water,
all the broken water that leaves
the dress empty, simply hanging from a tree.
She throws off the covers and the moon
washes her in a light that is disturbing,
lifts her into a restlessness
that coincides with the appearance of flies
earlier in the week dragging a net of a buzzing,
blue and claustrophobic,
forcing her to examine the roses.

The light says *hurry* and the boy
who came to the man and the woman late in marriage
slips his tooth under his parents' pillow.
In this way he knows they will remember to wake up.
He fills the night with his sweet breath,
breath unimpeded, flowing out of the space
once blocked by the tooth.

Behind the rock there is a cave.
Behind the moon there is simply dark space.
His mother will find the tooth when she makes the bed.
She will save it with all the other teeth hidden under pillows —

broken and intact, smooth and milky—
petals and buttons,
slices of the star-shaped fruit,
shells found nesting in the crevice of pools.

Plum Crazy

KATE SONTAG

Wait until this year's plums
become last year's plums,

the ladder's ascension
an icy path in late January,

the bee-stung hand hidden
by a flurry of leaves, healed,

the moon an alabaster bowl
above bare branches picked

clean as your days are full
of rinsing, halving, stoning,

simmering pounds of sugar
with pounds of flesh

funneled into endless steaming
jars sealed, cooled, labeled, and

sent downstairs like too many
children in the kitchen at once,

the plum of his appetite
what you cultivate and crave

most in this life, so who cares
that the walls grow sticky with flecks

of blue skin, occasional pits
slide under stove and fridge,

stray plums roll like cat toys
onto the floor from overstuffed

pockets and topple out of old
ice cream buckets off the counter,

why worry that you never answer
the phone anymore or sort through

the mail, having gone plum
crazy in your own shambles

of a house, putting your plum
curse on anyone who dares come

within whiffing distance
of your open windows,

from the UPS man to the lady
who reads the electric meter

to neighbors in each direction,
all dreaming of your plum

jam, butter, chutney, catsup,
spices swirling across lawn

and prairie, seeping past orchard
and driveway, even runaway dogs

howling at the door for you
to let them in to lick your pots

and ladles, until enough is enough
and the prospect of loading

the dishwasher and mopping
linoleum, scum-scrubbing

toilets, tubs, and shower tiles,
feather-dusting miles of shelves

and tabletops, vacuuming
every rotten corner

of every room, stripping
overripe sheets and pillowcases

from disheveled beds,
even doing dirty

laundry again
seems delicious.

Household Muse

JOYCE SUTPHEN

All morning, I nurse some fretful sorrow.
I take down curtains that gray at gathered
edges, I pull out dusty screens and wash
windows with blue water and newspaper,
the way my mother taught me. I throw
heaps of clothing into the middle of rooms:
jeans, sweaters, sweatshirts, dresses, belts,
underwear, old nylons — things no one ever
wears, things worn and ripped, things so
ugly I could not give them away. I stuff
these things into bags and boxes and carry
them out to a corner of the garage where
I won't have to look at them, hardly at all.
I go back into the house and sprinkle white
powder into the bathtubs and the sinks and
watch it blue over the rusty film of stainless
steel and porcelain. I pour a cap of piny
cleaner into an empty ice-cream pail; it
steams a vinegary smell, sloshes green and soapy.
Soon I have buckets everywhere: disinfectant
in the bathrooms, wood cleaner by the cabinets,
ammonia water for the walls. But then
the wind changes, and I am all of a sudden
weary and aware of this great effort
to wash the memory of love away. The muse
has departed, leaving me with afternoon.
My hands find no more places to scrub,
no more drawers to open; the light no longer
lifts the dust, and the house is abandoned,
like a page half-written, a rhythm that falters.

Housekeeping

VIRGINIA CHASE SUTTON

was never discussed, only frozen dinners
occasionally baked to the tiny iced heart

or pork chops in a pan, raw and reckless
in the silent kitchen or dusty under the living room

couch. My mother's not domestic. Endless
Sunday afternoons she would visit from the hospital.

After last fall's stroke, bedridden,
trying to walk, to hold her head

still on her neck. A red plaid cookbook's
teaching me to make pot roast, directions

like the buttery taste of meat too long
in the oven. My father wants me at the hospital,

helping with her wig as it falls goofy over her forehead,
missing the long, loopy scar. *Can't*, I tell him,

this roast has to go in right now. What do we
know of multihued vegetables, shiny

pieces tucked beside the magenta meat? How
can we learn to live with her again,

silent, drowsy conversations,
her metal bedpan neat in a paper sack?

It's easier to learn to cook,
measuring what's required, following directions

to the correct platter and spoon. The table's set
with plastic dishes, dark sunbursts

flat as our dinnertime faces. These stiff people
eat plain meat and ordinary vegetables,

my disappointment of a Midwestern language.
I'll do dishes, I call, avoiding the return

trip. Last year, my home economics teacher
taught the eighth grade girls

that unspotted glassware equals domestic contentment.
You've got the knack, she said to me one afternoon,

my little make-believe kitchen
a gallery of pure light and clean pots.

Coming Home

ELIZABETH TIBBETTS

Oh, God, the full-faced moon is smiling at me
in his pink sky, and I am alive, alive (!)
and driving home to you and our new refrigerator.
A skin of snow shines on the mountain beyond Burger King
and this garden of wires and poles and lighted signs.
Oh, I want to be new, I want to be the girl I saw
last night at the mike, sex leaking from her fingertips
as they traveled down to pick at her hem.
She was younger than I've ever been, with hair cropped,
ragged clothes, and face as clear as a child's.
She read as though she were in bed, eyes half closed,
teeth glistening, her shimmering body written
beneath her dress. She held every man in the audience
taut, and I thought of you. Now I'm coming home
dressed in my sensible coat and shoes, my purse
and a bundle of groceries beside me. When I arrive
we'll open the door of our Frigidaire
to its shining white interior, fill the butter's
little box, set eggs in their hollows, slip meats
and greens into separate drawers, and pause
in the newness of the refrigerator's light
while beside us, through the window,
the moon will lay a sheet on the kitchen floor.

Hospital Corners

ALISON TOWNSEND

Because it was the first thing
about housework my mother taught me,
and because it was all I knew to do
those blank weeks after she died,
I made my bed every morning, drawing
the rumpled sheet flat and tight
from the top down, then making hospital
corners, folding it in the neat,
diagonal V she'd learned in the Red Cross
and showed to me. She'd made it look easy,
flicking the linen she'd bleached
with Clorox and hung to dry in sun.
And it was when we did it together,
our hands moving in tandem as I copied
her movements, the pleasure of doing
what she did all I needed to recall who I was.
Alone by my maple spool bed,
I'd move from one side to the other,
pretending she was there,
until she somehow was, the January
room brimming with light
I had no word for but *angel*.

Together we'd draw the top sheet up,
turning the hem side down in a neat
cuff over the mohair blanket,
then pulling the spread up and over
in a kind of envelope that held
the pillow, slapping the fold
straight with the edge of our hand.
We folded the pink coverlet she'd
made for me last, in accordion pleats
I could unfurl in one smooth line,
as I got into bed at night and lay there,
mussing the taut sheets
with the sleep and tears of the living,

waiting for morning,
when she would come again, calming me
with those simple, familiar motions
that melted the world and dazzled me
with their brightness, making it possible
to do something almost like going on.

Western Holly Stove

ALISON TOWNSEND

Sometimes, when I'm cooking in autumn,
hovering, as I do now, to stir "Lentils
Monastery Style" (from the original *Diet*
for a Small Planet), over the weird hearth
of my electric, ceramic flat-top Admiral range —
its recessed coils glowing like red carp
trapped in black ice — I think of the stove
I had in my 20s and 30s. It was gas,
a Western Holly dating
from the Second World War or even before,
tucked in beneath the steep, knotty pine eaves
of that carriage house-cum-apartment
a friend once described
as a roll-top desk with windows.

The stove was white enamel
with a black top and hood,
where I arranged a cheap print by Pissarro
and my mother-in-law's hand-me-down spice jars,
wondering what mace and turmeric
were really for. The pilot was always out,
so you had to use a match,
the burners flaring up in a cockscomb
of fire that popped as it took,
a flame fish snapping
at the kiss of the Blue Tip.

I'd grown up cooking dinners for seven —
meat loaf, lasagna, fried chicken —
but it was there I really learned,
the stained pages of *Diet*,
The Vegetarian Epicure, and *Moosewood*
open on the Holly's convenient side counter,
as I stirred myself into being
someone cooler than I really was —
a real, live Californian flipping her

waist-length hair back over her shoulder
as she bent to taste soup.
Each July, when the apricot tree
in the backyard exploded
with saffron-colored fruit,
we made jam, standing for hours
over the golden goo ladled
into quart-sized jars we gave
everyone at Christmas.

When I cleaned the stove,
I got almost inside it,
holding my breath as I painted
its greasy, speckled enamel maw
with original Easy-Off
(so toxic it's now off the market),
or stood at the sink, scrubbing
its indestructible iron burners with Comet
until my hands were raw and I was lost
in the moment, happy at the sight of Mount Baldy's
snow-covered peak through the window.

The stove wasn't mine to take
so I left it behind when we moved to Oregon
and my first electric range.
But sometimes I dream of it still,
little stove we sometimes lit
to warm the kitchen in that mild place,
companionable presence with its hiss
of flame that burned blue and gold
and seemed to cook everything perfectly,
gilding it — the way the present
gilds the past — with nostalgia,
sweet and sticky as apricot jam,
as the raised black script of the words
"Western Holly" beneath my fingers
as I wiped the stove down after supper.

Date Nut Bread

ANN TOWNSEND

Not the recipe grandmother slipped the girl
who fell into marriage with the neighborhood bully.

Not the bread my mother offered at Christmas
to the Sisters in compensation for my misconduct.

Not that walnut-filled loaf, broken outside in spring,
crumbs fallen to the grass, each letting-the-world-go-by day

lapsing into another, as such days do —
not the bread sent in good-will, in recompense, or pride;

but this, heretic bread, recipe from the side of a box of dates.
Ingredients without history gather around my stove,

a package of fruit sliced open neatly
through the center, dark clotted beauties revealed

in their little casket of cardboard. And this:
dough licked from the spoon, slick egg, sugar, nutmeg,

and the taste, already, of the finished loaf,
from the mere dexterity of my hands, their greed

and generosity, their way of rescuing
what I still cannot name, but know will be good.

Day's End

ANN TOWNSEND

Once again
        I wipe the bedspread
down with a sponge,
        damp to catch the cat's hairs
where he lounges
        all afternoon, though had
I caught him
        I would have banished him
before you come home
        to sit near the pillows,
remove your shoes,
        and notice the minute
hairs where your head
        will rest and say *Jesus,*
will you look at this.
        It's in that kind of hurry
that I finish and vow
        to do better,
that I sweep the smudge
        of black and white hair
into the trash, that I pass
        quickly through two rooms
and sit at my desk
        as the door swings
open and you see me
        lingering, turning the pages
of the latest novel.

The Dinner Guest

ANN TOWNSEND

Let's begin with dinner, the menu:
      oiled lettuce, lemon juice, broken bread,

noodles spun with crushed tomatoes,
      and the matchstick julienne
            of fennel and skin of an orange.

I'm not angry yet, stirring the sauce.
      The wine tastes like a ripe field.

Let the fly rub his legs together
      over the wet cutting board,
            let him hold still in the bright aroma.

Dinner's next: sipping, chewing,
      talk of a high order among the men.

The female side of the table
      is motherly, leaning with spoons
            to serve the salad. No one says thanks —

is this 1953? Sorry.
      The newest year's dashed outside,

wind takes the trees,
      and pine needles fly, a dry shower,
            a needle storm. There's no decorum outside.

Stirring, stirring more sauce,
      while his words cascade around me,

I focus on the spoon,
      ruined with red. The spoon
            is the center of the rising heat world.

The spoon with its shreds of red
      holds the glory of taste and submission

in its olive grain.
        Bump, bump, bump, I tap the spoon
           on the bowl's edge.

I keep undercutting the beauty.
        The guest is sated, sips his wine,

tips the chair on two legs.
        The fly has found the leftovers.
           Let him eat from the same plate.

Domestic Work, 1937

NATASHA TRETHEWEY

All week she's cleaned
someone else's house,
stared down her own face
in the shine of copper-
bottomed pots, polished
wood, toilets she'd pull
the lid to — that look saying

Let's make a change, girl.

But Sunday mornings are hers —
church clothes starched
and hanging, a record spinning
on the console, the whole house
dancing. She raises the shades,
washes the rooms in light,
buckets of water, Octagon soap.

Cleanliness is next to godliness . . .

Windows and doors flung wide,
curtains two-stepping
forward and back, neck bones
bumping in the pot, a choir
of clothes clapping on the line.

Nearer my God to Thee . . .

She beats time on the rugs,
blows dust from the broom
like dandelion spores, each one
a wish for something better.

Housekeeping

NATASHA TRETHEWEY

We mourn the broken things, chair legs
wrenched from their seats, chipped plates,
the threadbare clothes. We work the magic
of glue, drive the nails, mend the holes.
We save what we can, melt small pieces
of soap, gather fallen pecans, keep neck bones
for soup. Beating rugs against the house,
we watch dust, lit like stars, spreading
across the yard. Late afternoon, we draw
the blinds to cool the rooms, drive the bugs
out. My mother irons, singing, lost in reverie.
I mark the pages of a mail-order catalog,
listen for passing cars. All day we watch
for the mail, some news from a distant place.

The History of Women

LESLIE ULLMAN

after Jack Gilbert

The history of women sighs
from the iron across the empty sleeves,
the exacting collars,
and edges along the porch rail.
It rises in the arc of a jump rope
then dissolves in a flurry of rhyme,
step on a crack, break your mother's back. . . .
It sends some children home
to the table waiting to
be set for eight, away from the fragrant
dusk, away from the last secret
whispered between cupped hands.
Still, there are days when a girl
roams alone in her body, humming and
dreaming, a heroine among weeds and wildflowers.
When childhood ends, it is cut at the root
though for a time, the young beauties
spring lightly from buses to offices
without windows, thinking they
will always be pretty
and soon will leave town.
                          Understandable then
that marriage appears to them
as an offer. They mean to
accept. They mean to make
the best of it, swimming
in a current that keeps them
in one place, smoothing Oil of Olay
over their useful hands, comforting
their mothers whose sadness
ceases to baffle them.
They wave the last child into
the evening, the first in a string
of crucible nights, and try

not to pace at the window.
Divorce leaves them stunned, supple
as leather, stranded for a time
on a long path towards love.
                              At times they see beauty
in each other mirrored nowhere in the eyes
of men, or in movies they watch when they
can't sleep. Waiting in a long line
to vote, they sense the shape of themselves
briefly, like ice cubes dropped in a lake,
though the speeches have blurred
to a long hush, waves against sand;
so history drives them inward
with the sound of someone clearing his throat.
Then one day it wakes them up
in the middle of their lives,
in a house that smells of cinnamon
or woodsmoke, surrounded by a small wild yard.
Scrubbed apples drying on a cloth. The sun
just setting, gold over the valley's greens.
Silence everywhere, softening the horizon
and bringing it even closer.

Canning Cellar, Early Sixties

JUDITH VOLLMER

Only women went down
the stone steps
and opened the cupboard
for the muslin blouses & loose skirts.
Then they weren't women anymore,
braids disappeared into turbans & scarves.
In the hundred twenty degree heat
they bowed their shoulders,
they offered the skin of their fingerprints
to the galvanized tub & red coils.
The glint of knives over buckets of fruitpeel
was power they sharpened on leather
strops. Wet glass, the knives,
& silver teeth of old women —
They all shined.
They set their jaws
like horses numbed to the bit
and braced their ankles against chairs
braced in dirt. Time was nobody's
when tomatoes were dead ripe
and peaches & pears bruised to the touch
and beans multiplied in twelve rows of bushels.

Back to Catfish

BELLE WARING

The café with the hotwire
boys is where you are and me
I'm back to cooking catfish
with banana, disguised
as a Guadeloupean delicacy,
but it's still its old ugly-snout
self. Now when you *bon temps roulez,*
you booze in a fancy French joint
where the ladies get menus
with no price list. My little sun
king, who knows when you'll blow
in. A woman like me
with a fine arts degree
could have been a master
engraver. Counterfeiter.
Not the counterfeiter's moll.

Sure. I'm back to cooking
catfish, a creature with purpose
in life, to sweep the creek bottom
clean as the moon.
I'm waiting for thee,
wearing this swamp green
shirt you left. I could never
just throw it away,
the color of a hangover. A bruise.

But I could start without you.
Scarf up bananafish by myself.
Clean this kitchen with your keepsake
shirt, scrub every bad business
I can reach. Go out for some middlebrow
cappuccino. Swing by the Tastee Diner
for some brawl-proof pie. I'll smile
when I'm ready and feel
complete. Who knows who I might meet?

I could swim the night in my cherry Nova
and sweep down the state road
crossing the river
on its long goddamn way home.

The Lady on the Cover of *Family Circle*

INGRID WENDT

isn't with her family or anyone
else by this time, except you
know she's waiting
for something: leaning

expectant against the white
wrought iron railing, the garden
you'd never know she works in off
to her right, to her left the house
where maybe her family waits

for her
to become what she got through her day for: the moment
when none of her daily life shows.

Notice her dress, that's part
of it, how long it took to embroider all
those flowers from neck to waist to floor.

Notice her hair, her careful
eyes, the gloss
on her lips, cheeks, untouched
by the steam of dishes or diapers or
ironing or bathing and planning just right so
it won't all fall apart.

Nothing surprises her. Not weather,
dirt, husband, herself.
Her children obey her like keys.

See how she watches you, waiting
to see if you will
notice her disdain,
her knowledge that once you do

notice her there
is nothing left for her to do,

there is no one
left to respect.

Starting from Scratch

INGRID WENDT

To begin with, none of your neighbors began here.
Everyone moved in years before you moved into
a pattern you found yourself part of
before you intended: flowers, fences,
attention to details your mother always took care of,
duller than film on dishes it was always your job to wipe.
Nobody spoke about courage.

Nobody said you could choose this life.
It happened, it didn't, the fact
you could choose to remain would become
what's yours to control: hours
of sleeping and waking, meals, the home
you need to go out in the world from.
Neighborhood customs you know you can count on.

Recipes, grapes exchanged for zucchini, the garden
someone will know when to plant.
The book you suggest. The pattern of limits
no one has asked for, told over coffee, lives
like yours you could have become
starting from scratch. Each day
the way you will live before what comes next.

Quilt

VALERIE WOHLFELD

Patchwork-paneled the mitered heart remade.
Each cloth mosaic pin-stabbed as rare moths.
Scrap-built, spliced, rimmed in tattered errant threads,
then savage edges tucked under. From plundered
velvets snipped from cocktail dresses and silks
scissored from neckties, appear the opened
spouts of venae cavae and aortae.
Mock hearted miraculous shroud, I sleep
ventricle to ventricle: one satin —
one cellular-walled, blood-sated, tendoned,
valved: I sleep aorta to aorta:
great branched, arched vessel under one brocade;
— heart to Siamese heart I sleep in monstrous sleep.

The heart's vacant caverns, hollow-structured,
loom-strung in muscle-fibered stalactites
and stalagmites; veins blood-silted, venules'
tributary-twistings; fish-mouthed valves' sea-
swallowings; contracted shot of current
mistaking electricity for murmured
immortality; beats allocated
to the hangman roping the heart's debris
— beats uncounted as glass baubles pouring
through the fingers of a bead stringer, beads
of paste and paper, too, beside the glass:
— my mother, sewing, sang with the heart singing
too, remnant-winged in motley ravening.

Cribbed heart outlined in buttonhole stitches.
Goggled eyes of French knots dotted atriums
left and right. Into the needle's sly slit
my mother passed the beeswax-rolled thread. Would the cloth
sweeten from the bees' labor, their clover
and asters? She sprinkled cinnamon
in each fabric quadrant, through translucent
stencils, guiding the quilting. A cosmos

of spice and bees, nebula of satin-
salvaged chambers: the silvered needle, laced —
mysterious forged eye sighted for the purblind
dagger — to wound and bind, to slice every
convolute secret of the sutured heart,
 — and with the sutured heart still singing.

Prayer

CAROLYNE WRIGHT

Bless my life — its inks
and paperweights and houseplants
fringed with sun.
Give me the quiet, Lord,
I close my eyes
and turn my tongue back for.
Don't feed me too much,
and when I can't decide between love
and what's jammed in the typewriter
or roughed out on the drawing board,
take away the coins I flip
and make me listen: That young man
smiling in my kitchen at me is in love.
With me. That's one door in my house
that opens on more than grief
or dirty sheets or the supermarket
twice a week. It gives on light,
and I, your moth, am beating to get in.
Give us this day, and with no promises
but what we are — two small people
trying to be one — send us out
and say, "That's fine. Light fills your gaps.
Breathe on."

Contributors' Notes

ELIZABETH ALEXANDER is the author of three collections of poetry, most recently *Antebellum Dream Book*, as well as *The Black Interior*, a collection of essays on contemporary African American artistic life through literature, paintings, film, and popular media. Alexander currently teaches English and American Studies at Yale University.

JULIA ALVAREZ'S novels include *How the Garcia Girls Lost Their Accents*, *In the Time of the Butterflies*, *Yo!*, and *In the Name of Salomé*. Her most recent book of poems is *The Woman I Kept to Myself*. Other books of poetry include *The Housekeeping Book*, *The Other Side/ El Otro Lado*, and *Homecoming: New and Selected Poems*. *Something to Declare*, a book of essays, was published in 1998. Alvarez has also authored several books for young readers.

GINGER ANDREWS was born and raised in North Bend, Oregon, and lives there still. She is the author of two poetry collections, *Hurricane Sisters* and *An Honest Answer*. She runs a small housecleaning business with her three sisters, who all live within walking distance.

MARGARET ATWOOD'S books have been published in more than thirty-five countries. She is the author of more than thirty books of fiction, poetry, and critical essays. In addition to *The Handmaid's Tale*, her novels include *Cat's Eye* — shortlisted for the Booker Prize; *Alias Grace*, which won the Giller Prize in Canada and the Premio Mondello in Italy; *The Blind Assassin*, winner of the 2000 Booker Prize; and most recently *Oryx and Crake*. She lives in Toronto with writer Graeme Gibson.

JULIANNA BAGGOTT is the best-selling author of three novels, *Girl Talk*, *The Miss America Family*, and *The Madam*, as well as a book of poems, *This Country of Mothers*. A collaborative novel with Steve Almond, titled *Which Brings Me to You: A Novel in Confessions*, is forthcoming. *The Anybodies*, the first in a series of young adult novels, was published under her pen name, N. E. Bode, in 2004.

DOROTHY BARRESI'S newest book of poetry is *Rouge Pulp*. Her first book, *All of the Above*, won the 1990 Barnard New Women Poets Prize, and her second, *The Post-Rapture Diner*, won an American Book Award in 1997. She has been the recipient of a National Endowment for the Arts Fellowship, two Pushcart Prizes, and the Emily Clark Balch Poetry Prize. She is a professor of English at California State University–Northridge and lives in Los Angeles with her husband and two sons.

JAN BEATTY'S newest book is *Boneshaker*. She is also the author of *Mad River*, winner of the 1994 Agnes Lynch Starrett Poetry Prize, and *Ravenous*, winner of the 1995 State Street Chapbook Prize. Her poetry appears in numerous publications and anthologies.

KIMBERLY BLAESER, an associate professor of English at the University of Wisconsin–Milwaukee, teaches Native American literature and creative writing. Her publications include two collections of poetry, *Trailing You*, which won the 1993 First Book Award from the Native Writers' Circle of the Americas, and *Absentee Indians and Other Poems*. She is also the author of a critical study, *Gerald Vizenor: Writing in the Oral Tradition*, and the editor of two anthologies, *Stories Migrating Home: A Collection of Anishinabe Prose* and *Traces in Blood, Bone, and Stone: Contemporary Ojibwe Poetry*.

MARIANNE BORUCH is the author of five poetry collections, most recently *Poems New and Selected*. She has also published a collection of essays in the University of Michigan's "Poets on Poetry" series, *Poetry's Old Air*. Another essay collection, *In the Blue Pharmacy*, is forthcoming. Her awards include two National Endowment for the Arts Fellowships and two Pushcart Prizes. She teaches in the MFA program at Purdue University.

JILL BRECKENRIDGE won the Bluestem Award, judged by William Stafford, for her book of poems, *How to Be Lucky*. Her sequence of poetry and prose about the Civil War, *Civil Blood*, was nominated for a National Book Critics Circle Award and the American Library Association's Notable Books of the Year. Her awards include Loft-McKnight Writers' Awards in both creative prose and poetry, a Bush Foundation Fellowship, and two Minnesota State Arts Board grants. She has recently completed another collection of poems and is working on a memoir.

JEANNE BRYNER is the author of the poetry collections *Breathless* and *Blind Horse* and the fiction work *Eclipse: Stories*. She has also written *Tenderly Lift Me: Nurses Honored, Celebrated, and Remembered*. Bryner has received fellowships from the Younger Poets Seminar at Bucknell University and from the Ohio Arts Council. Her poetry has been adapted for stage, and her play about the lives of nurses, *Intensive Care*, was recently part of the International Fringe Festival in Edinburgh, Scotland.

VICTORIA CHANG'S first book of poetry, *Circle*, won the Crab Orchard Review Award Series in Poetry. Her poems have appeared in such journals as the *Nation*, *Poetry*, *Threepenny Review*, *Kenyon Review*, *Virginia Quarterly Review*, and *Slate*. She is also the editor of *Asian American Poetry: The Next Generation*. She resides in Los Angeles and San Diego.

MARILYN CHIN was born in Hong Kong and raised in Portland, Oregon. Her latest book of poetry is *Rhapsody in Plain Yellow*. She is also the author of *The Phoenix Gone, the Terrace Empty*, winner of the PEN Josephine Miles Award, and *Dwarf Bamboo*. Her poetry has appeared in the *Iowa Review*, the *Paris Review*, *Parnassus*, and many other journals. Two National Endowment for the Arts Fellowships, two Fulbright Fellowships, a Stegner Fellowship, four Pushcart Prizes, and a Mary Roberts Rinehart Award are among her many honors.

SANDRA CISNEROS'S latest novel is *Caramelo*. She is also the author of *The House on Mango Street* and *Woman Hollering Creek* and the poetry collections *My Wicked, Wicked Ways* and *Loose Woman*. Her many awards include a MacArthur Foundation Fellowship.

LUCILLE CLIFTON'S *Blessing the Boats: New and Selected Poems 1988–2000* was a National Book Award winner. *The Terrible Stories* was a National Book Award nominee.

Good Woman: Poems and a Memoir 1969–1980 was nominated for the Pulitzer Prize; *Two-Headed Woman* was also a Pulitzer Prize nominee and winner of the University of Massachusetts Press Juniper Prize. Other books by Clifton are *The Book of Light*; *Quilting: Poems 1987–1990*; *Next: New Poems*; *An Ordinary Woman*; *Good News About the Earth*; and *Good Times*. She has also written *Generations: A Memoir* and several books for children.

GERALDINE CONNOLLY serves as codirector of Plum Writers Retreat. She has won two National Endowment for the Arts Fellowships in poetry, as well as the Margaret Bridgman Fellowship of the Bread Loaf Writers' Conference and the W. B. Yeats Society of New York Poetry Prize. Her work has appeared in many anthologies and was selected for the *Poetry 180 Anthology* by Billy Collins. Her books include *Food for the Winter* and *Province of Fire*. She divides her time between Washington, D.C., and Montana.

BARBARA CROOKER has published poems in periodicals such as *Yankee*, the *Christian Science Monitor*, and the *Denver Quarterly*, and she has published eleven chapbooks. Her work has also been anthologized in *Worlds in Their Words* and *Boomer Girls*. Her grants and awards include three Pennsylvania Council on the Humanities Fellowships in literature, the W. B. Yeats Society of New York Prize, and the Thomas Merton Poetry of the Sacred Award. She has a poster in her front hall that reads, "Dull Women Have Immaculate Houses."

DEBORAH DIGGES attended the Iowa Writers' Workshop, where she was awarded a teaching-writing fellowship and an MFA in poetry. Digges has published three books of poems and two memoirs, the most recent *The Stardust Lounge: Stories from a Boy's Adolescence*. Her work has received many awards, among them the Delmore Schwartz Memorial Prize, The Kingsely Tufts Prize, and a Guggenheim Fellowship. A new collection of poems, *Trapeze*, is forthcoming.

AMY DRYANSKY, author of *How I Got Lost So Close to Home*, has published poems in the *Harvard Review, DoubleTake, Green Mountains Review*, and many other journals. Her honors include a grant from the Ludwig Vogelstein Foundation and a Pushcart Prize nomination.

DENISE DUHAMEL'S most recent books are *Two and Two* and *Queen for a Day: Selected and New Poems*. She has recently coedited, with Maureen Seaton and David Trinidad, *Saints of Hysteria: A Half-Century of Collaborative American Poetry*.

HEID ERDRICH is the author of *Fishing for Myth*, a Minnesota Voices Project winner. She is also coeditor of *Sister Nations: Native American Women Writers on Community*. The recipient of a Bush Leadership Fellowship and a Minnesota Book Award, she teaches at the University of St. Thomas in St. Paul, Minnesota.

SUSAN FIRER is the author of four books of poetry. Her third, *The Lives of the Saints and Everything*, won the Cleveland State Poetry Center Prize and the Posner Award. Her most recent book, *The Laugh We Make When We Fall*, won the 2001 Backwaters Prize. Her work has appeared in *The Best American Poetry* as well as in *Chicago Review, New American Writing, Iowa Review*, and many other journals.

DIANE GILLIAM FISHER is a graduate of the Warren Wilson College MFA Program for Writers. Her books include *Recipe for Blackberry Cake*, *One of Everything*, and *Kettle Bottom*, a collection of poems written in the voices of people living in the coal camps at the time of the West Virginia mine wars.

PAMELA GEMIN is the author of *Vendettas, Charms, and Prayers: Poems*, a Minnesota Voices Project winner, and editor and coeditor of *Are You Experienced?* and *Boomer Girls*, poetry anthologies from the University of Iowa Press. She teaches creative writing at the University of Wisconsin Oshkosh.

JOY HARJO'S latest book of poems is *How We Became Human*. Other poetry collections include *A Map to the Next World* and *The Woman Who Fell from the Sky*. She has written a book for children, *The Good Luck Cat*, and she is also an accomplished musician whose latest recording is titled *Native Joy for Real*.

HOLLY IGLESIAS is author of *Hands-On Saints* (poems) and a critical work, *Boxing Inside the Box: Women's Prose Poetry*. She recently completed a manuscript of poems on the 1994 World's Fair, *Now You See It*, and is working on the translation of *La Sucesión*, the most recent work of Cuban poet Caridad Atencio.

ANGELA JACKSON, a Chicago native, has published numerous collections of poetry and fiction, including *Voodoo/Love Magic*, *The Greenville Club*, *Solo in Boxcar Third Floor E*, *Dark Legs and Silk Kisses*, and a collected works edition of her poetry, *And All These Roads Be Luminous* (1998). She has received a National Endowment for the Arts Fellowship and an American Book Award.

ALLISON JOSEPH is the author of five books of poetry, including *Imitation of Life*, *In Every Seam*, and *Worldly Pleasures*. She lives, writes, and teaches in Carbondale, Illinois, where she serves on the creative writing program faculty at Southern Illinois University.

JULIA KASDORF'S latest book is *Eve's Striptease*. Her previous collection, *Sleeping Preacher*, was the winner of the 1991 Agnes Lynch Starrett Poetry Prize and the 1993 Great Lakes College Association Award for New Writing. She is also the author of *The Body and the Book: Writing from a Mennonite Life*, a collection of essays and poems, and her work has appeared in the *New Yorker*, *Paris Review*, and *Poetry*. She teaches at the Pennsylvania State University.

LAURA KASISCHKE is the author of six collections of poetry. Her latest, *Gardening in the Dark*, was preceded by *Dance and Disappear*, a Juniper Prize winner. She has also published three novels, most recently *The Life Before Her Eyes*. Kasischke's many honors include the Alice Fay diCastagnola Award from the Poetry Society of America, the Beatrice Hawley Award, the Pushcart Prize, and the Elmer Holmes Bobst Award for Emerging Writers. She teaches at the University of Michigan.

JOSIE KEARNS is the author of *New Numbers*, a book of poems, and a nonfiction work, *Life After the Line*. Her honors include grants from the Michigan Council for the Arts and Cultural Affairs, three Hopwood Awards, and the first McLeod-Grobe Prize from *Poetry Northwest*. A coeditor of *New Poems from the Third Coast*, she teaches writing and literature at the University of Michigan.

SARAH KENNEDY'S books include *Flow Blue, Double Exposure,* and *Consider the Lilies.* She is book review editor for *Shenandoah* and teaches creative writing and Renaissance literature at Mary Baldwin College in Staunton, Virginia.

JESSE LEE KERCHEVAL was born in France and raised in Florida. She is the author of six books, including the novel *The Museum of Happiness,* the memoir *Space,* and the poetry collections *World as Dictionary* and *Dog Angel.* She teaches at the University of Wisconsin at Madison, where she directs the Wisconsin Institute for Creative Writing.

JULIE KING is poetry editor for the online journal *Eclectica.* Recent poems have appeared in *Primavera, Puerto del Sol,* and *Quarterly West.* She has also written, directed, and produced a short film, *Worlds,* and has starred in two B horror films. She lives with her husband, Tom, and their four cats and teaches poetry at the University of Wisconsin–Parkside.

KRISTIN KOVACIC is the editor of *Birth: A Literary Companion* (University of Iowa Press). Her poetry and fiction have appeared in numerous publications, including *Brain, Child Magazine, Puerto del Sol,* the *Cimarron Review, Gulf Stream,* and *Third Coast.* Her work has been recognized by the Academy of American Poets, and she is the recipient of a fellowship in poetry from the Pennsylvania Council on the Arts. She teaches in the MFA program at Chatham College and in the literary arts department of the Pittsburgh High School for the Creative and Performing Arts.

LAURIE KUTCHINS is the author of two books of poetry—*Between Towns* and *The Night Path.* She has recently completed a new book of poetry and is working on a book of lyric nonfiction. Her poems and essays have appeared in such publications as the *Southern Review, Ploughshares,* the *Georgia Review,* the *New Yorker, Poetry,* and the *Kenyon Review.* She teaches at James Madison University in Virginia.

ESTELLA LAUTER is professor emerita in the Department of English at the University of Wisconsin Oshkosh after a career of interdisciplinary work in women's studies, aesthetics, and the new literatures. She began to write and publish poems after her second child was born. She belongs to the generation of women who thought we had to do it all at once.

DORIANNE LAUX is the author of three collections of poetry: *Smoke, What We Carry,* and *Awake.* With Kim Addonizio, she is also coauthor of *The Poet's Companion: A Guide to the Pleasures of Writing Poetry.* Among her awards are a Pushcart Prize, an Editor's Choice III Award, and a fellowship from the National Endowment for the Arts. Laux is an associate professor at the University of Oregon's Program in Creative Writing.

LISA LEWIS is the author of *The Unbeliever* and *Silent Treatment.* Recent work has appeared in *Crab Orchard Review,* the *Michigan Quarterly Review,* the *Journal, Many Mountains Moving,* and the *Florida Review.* Lewis directs the creative writing program at Oklahoma State University.

DIANE LOCKWARD is the author of *Eve's Red Dress,* a book of poetry. Her poems have most recently appeared in the *Beloit Poetry Journal, North American Review,* and *Prairie*

Schooner. Her work has also been featured on *Poetry Daily* and read by Garrison Keillor on *The Writer's Almanac.* Lockward is the recipient of a 2003 Poetry Fellowship from the New Jersey State Council on the Arts.

GAIL MARTIN is the author of *The Hourglass Heart,* a collection of poetry. Her work has appeared in numerous journals including *Folio, Poetry Northwest, Primavera,* and *Rattle.* She recently completed her master's degree in clinical social work. Selected by Alice Fulton as winner of the 1999 Poet Hunt sponsored by the *MacGuffin,* she lives with her husband and daughters in Kalamazoo, Michigan.

SHARA MC CALLUM is the author of two books of poems, *Song of Thieves* and *The Water Between Us,* winner of the 1998 Agnes Lynch Starrett Poetry Prize. Her poems and personal essays appear in numerous journals and anthologies. She is the director of the Stadler Center for Poetry and teaches at Bucknell University and in the Stonecoast low-residency MFA program. McCallum lives with her family in Lewisburg, Pennsylvania.

PAULA MC LAIN received her MFA in poetry from the University of Michigan. She is the author of a memoir, *Like Family: Growing Up in Other People's Houses,* and a collection of poetry, *Less of Her.* Her poems have appeared in numerous journals and anthologies. She lives in Madison, Wisconsin.

JANE MEAD is the author of *House of Poured-Out Waters* and *The Lord and the General Din of the World.* A recipient of awards and fellowships from the Whiting, Lannan, and Guggenheim foundations, she is poet-in-residence at Wake Forest University and also teaches in the low-residency MFA program at New England College and at the Iowa Summer Writing Festival.

SARAH MESSER teaches poetry and creative nonfiction at the University of North Carolina in Wilmington. She is also the author of a book of poems, *Bandit Letters,* and a memoir, *Red House.*

LESLIE ADRIENNE MILLER'S most recent poetry collection is *Eat Quite Everything You See.* She is also the author of *Yesterday Had a Man in It, Ungodliness,* and *Staying Up for Love.* She is currently an associate professor of English at the University of St. Thomas in St. Paul, Minnesota.

LAUREL MILLS is the author of four books of poetry, including *I Sing Back* and *The Gull Is My Divining Rod.* Her poems have appeared in *Ms.,* the *Kenyon Review,* and *Calyx,* and she has written a novel, *Undercurrents.*

KYOKO MORI was raised in Kobe, Japan. Her first novel for young adults, *Shizuko's Daughter,* was followed by a collection of poetry, *Fallout.* She is also the author of a memoir, *The Dream of Water;* a book of essays, *Polite Lies,* about her life as a Japanese American woman in the Midwest; and *Stone Field, True Arrow,* a novel.

SHARON OLDS'S many honors include a National Endowment for the Arts grant; a Guggenheim Foundation Fellowship; the San Francisco Poetry Center Award for her first collection, *Satan Says;* and the Lamont Poetry Selection and the National Book Critics Circle Award for *The Dead and the Living.* Her other books of poetry are *Blood, Tin,*

Straw; The Gold Cell; The Wellspring; and *The Father.* Olds teaches poetry workshops at New York University's Graduate Creative Writing Program, along with a workshop at Goldwater Hospital on Roosevelt Island in New York. She lives in New York City.

ALICIA SUSKIN OSTRIKER is one of America's best-known poets and critics. Her most recent book of poems is *The Volcano Sequence.* She is also the author of nine previous volumes of poetry, including *The Crack in Everything* and *Little Space: Poems Selected and New, 1968–1998,* both finalists for the National Book Award, and *The Imaginary Lover,* winner of the William Carlos Williams Award.

GAILMARIE PAHMEIER is the author of *The House on Breakaheart Road.* She is the recipient of numerous writing awards, including the Chambers Memorial Award in Poetry and the Witter Bynner Foundation Poetry Fellowship. She coordinates the creative writing program at the University of Nevada, Reno.

PEGGY PENN, author of *So Close,* directs a project on the use of writing in treating chronic illnesses and trauma at the Ackerman Institute for the Family. She lectures and consults throughout the United States and Europe and is the coauthor of *Milan Systemic Family Therapy: Conversations in Theory and Practice.* Her poetry has been published in numerous journals, and she is currently working on a book on writing and psychotherapy. She is married to Arthur Penn; they have two children and four grandchildren.

ZARINA MULLAN PLATH has received awards from the Illinois Arts Council, and as a graduate student she was one of two in the nation to receive a Ruth Lilly Fellowship. Her poetry has appeared in such journals as the *Caribbean Writer, Whetstone,* and *Faultline.* She teaches part-time at Illinois Wesleyan University, writes for the nonprofit agency Parents' Choice, and is at work on a children's book. Ms. Plath, who is half Indian, lives with her husband and children in central Illinois.

MARTHA RHODES is the author of three poetry collections: *Mother Quiet; Perfect Disappearance,* winner of the 2000 Green Rose Prize from New Issues Press; and *At the Gate.* She teaches at Sarah Lawrence College and in the Warren Wilson College MFA Program for Writers. She is also the director of Four Way Books.

NATASHA SAJÉ'S two books of poetry are *Red Under the Skin* and *Bend.* She has also published many essays and reviews. Her honors include a Fulbright grant, the Campbell Corner Poetry Prize, and the Robert Winner award from the Poetry Society of America. She teaches at Westminster College in Salt Lake City and in the Vermont College MFA in Writing Program.

JANE SATTERFIELD'S poetry collections are *Assignation at Vanishing Point* and *Shepherdess with an Automatic.* A Pushcart Prize nominee for poetry and the essay, she is the recipient of numerous awards, including a John Atherton Scholarship in Poetry at Bread Loaf and the Heekin Foundation's Cuchulain Prize for Rhetoric in the Essay. Her poems and prose have appeared in such journals as *American Poetry Review, Antioch Review,* the *American Voice,* and *Quarterly West.* Born in England and educated in the United States, she is an assistant professor at Loyola College in Maryland.

MAUREEN SEATON'S fifth collection of poetry is *Venus Examines Her Breast*. She is also the author of *Little Ice Age, Furious Cooking, The Sea among the Cupboards*, and *Fear of Subways*, as well as collaborative writing projects with Denise Duhamel. She directs the creative writing program at the University of Miami.

HEATHER SELLERS is the author of two volumes of poetry, most recently *Drinking Girls and Their Dresses*. Her story collection, *Georgia Underwater*, won a Barnes and Noble Discover Great New Writers Award, and she has just finished a memoir of the writing life, *Page after Page*. The recipient of a National Endowment for the Arts Fellowship, Sellers is also a children's book writer; *Spike and Cubby's Ice Cream Island Adventure!* is her first in a series. In addition, she has recently finished a novel, *Women Who Run*, and is at work on a memoir.

PAULA SERGI is coeditor of *Boomer Girls: Poems by Women from the Baby Boom Generation* (University of Iowa Press, 1999). She received a Wisconsin Arts Board Artist Fellowship in 2001 and has recently been selected for artist residencies at the Virginia Center for the Creative Arts and the Ragdale Foundation. Her poetry is published regularly, in such journals as *Primavera, Crab Orchard Review*, and *Spoon River Poetry Review*. A graduate of the University of Wisconsin at Madison, she has a bachelor of science degree in nursing and worked in home health and public health nursing for ten years. She received an MFA in creative writing from Vermont College.

DIANE SEUSS, writer in residence at Kalamazoo College, is the author of *It Blows You Hollow*. Recent work has appeared in *Artful Dodge*, the *Georgia Review*, the *North American Poetry Review*, and *Rattle*, and has been anthologized in *Boomer Girls, Are You Experienced?, New Poems from the Third Coast*, and *September 11: American Writers Respond*. Her poem "Falling Man" is part of a song cycle about September 11 — "Requiem" — by composer H. J. Thoms. Seuss won the Allen Ginsberg Memorial Prize in 2000.

FAITH SHEARIN'S *The Owl Question* won the May Swenson Poetry Award. She has been a fellow at the Fine Arts Work Center in Provincetown and writer-in-residence at Interlochen Arts Academy, and her poems have appeared in such journals as *Ploughshares, Chicago Review*, and *Poetry Northwest*. Shearin earned an MFA at Sarah Lawrence College, and she lives with her husband and daughter in southern Michigan.

CATHY SONG'S most recent book of poems is *The Land of Bliss*. She is also the author of *School Figures, Picture Bride*, and *Frameless Windows, Squares of Light*. Her awards include a Yale Younger Poets Prize and a National Endowment for the Arts Fellowship. She lives with her family in Honolulu.

KATE SONTAG is coeditor of *After Confession: Poetry as Autobiography*. Her poems have been featured in *Valparaiso Poetry Review* and have appeared in many other journals and anthologies. She teaches at Ripon College.

JOYCE SUTPHEN lives in Chaska, Minnesota, and teaches at Gustavus Adolphus College in St. Peter, Minnesota. Her poems have appeared in *Poetry, Hayden's Ferry*, and *Gettysburg Review*. Her first book, *Straight Out of View*, won the Barnard New Women

Poets Prize. Her second book, *Coming Back to the Body*, was a Minnesota Book Award finalist, and her third book, *Naming the Stars*, was recently published.

VIRGINIA CHASE SUTTON'S first book of poetry is titled *Embellishments*. Her poems have appeared in *Antioch Review, Paris Review, Witness*, and many other publications. Her many awards include a Bread Loaf scholarship and finalist titles for the National Poetry Series and other competitions. Recently completed are *Never Construct Narrative* and *Reading Electra to Sleep*, two new poetry manuscripts.

ELIZABETH TIBBETTS'S book *In the Well* won the 2002 Bluestem Poetry Award. Her work has appeared in such journals as the *American Scholar, Green Mountains Review*, and *Prairie Schooner*. She received a 2003 Maine Arts Commission Fellowship, and her work has been nominated for the Pushcart Prize. She lives in Maine and works as a nurse.

ALISON TOWNSEND is the author of two books of poetry, *The Blue Dress* and *What the Body Knows*. Her poetry and essays have appeared in *Crazyhorse, Fourth Genre*, the *North American Review*, the *Southern Review*, and *Under the Sun*, among many others. She lives in the farm country outside Madison, Wisconsin, and teaches English and creative writing at the University of Wisconsin–Whitewater.

ANN TOWNSEND is the author of two collections of poetry, *The Coronary Garden* and *Dime Store Erotics*. She is the recipient of grants from the Ohio Arts Council and the National Endowment for the Arts, and she has also been awarded the Discovery Prize from the *Nation*. Her poems have appeared widely in journals and anthologies. An associate professor of English at Denison University, Townsend lives in Granville, Ohio.

NATASHA TRETHEWEY was born in Gulfport, Mississippi. Her first poetry collection, *Domestic Work*, won the inaugural 1999 Cave Canem Poetry Prize. Her second collection, *Bellocq's Ophelia*, was named a 2003 Notable Book by the American Library Association. Trethewey lives in Decatur, Georgia, and is an assistant professor of creative writing at Emory University.

LESLIE ULLMAN'S *Slow Work through Sand* won the Iowa Poetry Prize in 1997. She is also the author of *Dreams by No One's Daughter* and *Natural Histories*, winner of a Yale Younger Poets Award. A two-time National Endowment for the Arts Fellow, Ullman directs the creative writing program at the University of Texas–El Paso.

JUDITH VOLLMER'S newest collection of poems is *Reactor*. Her other books include *The Door Open to the Fire, Black Butterfly*, and *Level Green*. She lives in Pittsburgh and directs the writing program at the University of Pittsburgh at Greensburg.

BELLE WARING'S first book of poems, *Refuge*, won the Associated Writing Programs' Award for Poetry in 1989 and the Washington Prize in 1991, and was cited by *Publishers Weekly* as one of the best books of 1990. Her newest book is *Dark Blonde*, which won the Levis Reading Prize in 1998. Waring currently teaches creative writing at Children's Hospital in Washington, D.C.

INGRID WENDT'S first book of poems, *Moving the House,* grew out of the experience of saving an old house from demolition at the hands of the McDonald's hamburger chain. She is the author of three other books of poems, two anthologies, and a teaching guide. Her most recent book, *The Angle of Sharpest Ascending,* received the 2003 Yellowglen Prize. A recent Fulbright Senior Specialist in Germany, she lives in Eugene, Oregon.

VALERIE WOHLFELD'S 1994 collection, *Thinking the World Visible,* won the Yale Series of Younger Poets Prize. She has published poems in the *Antioch Review, New England Review,* the *New Yorker,* and *Prairie Schooner.* She has just completed a second manuscript, *The Dreams of an Imaginary Woman,* a compilation of poetry and prose.

CAROLYNE WRIGHT has published three books and four chapbooks of poetry, including *Premonitions of an Uneasy Guest,* three volumes of poetry translated from Spanish and Bengali, and a collection of essays. Her most recent collection, *Seasons of Mangoes and Brainfire,* won the Blue Lynx Poetry Prize, the Oklahoma Book Award in Poetry, and an American Book Award from the Before Columbus Foundation. Forthcoming are a new collection, *A Change of Maps,* and *Majestic Nights: Love Poems by Bengali Women.* She lives in Cleveland, where she teaches at Cleveland State University.

Permissions

Alexander, Elizabeth. "The female seer will burn upon this pyre," from *Antebellum Dream Book*, Graywolf Press, 2001. Copyright © 2001 by Elizabeth Alexander. Reprinted by permission of Graywolf Press, St. Paul, Minnesota.

Alvarez, Julia. "How I Learned to Sweep." From *Homecoming*. Copyright © 1984 by Julia Alvarez. Published by Plume, an imprint of Dutton Signet, a division of Penguin Books, USA, Inc.; originally published by Grove Press. Reprinted by permission of Susan Bergholz Literary Services, New York. All rights reserved.

Andrews, Ginger. "Down on My Knees," from *An Honest Answer*, Story Line Press, 1999. Copyright © 1999 by Story Line Press. "The Hurricane Sisters Work Regardless," from *Hurricane Sisters*, Story Line Press, 2004. Copyright © 2004 by Ginger Andrews. Both poems reprinted by permission of the author.

Atwood, Margaret. "Romantic," from *Morning in the Burned House: New Poems by Margaret Atwood*. Copyright © 1995 by Margaret Atwood. Reprinted by permission of Houghton Mifflin Company. All rights reserved.

Baggott, Julianna. "Kitchens: 1959," from *This Country of Mothers*, Southern Illinois University Press. Copyright © 2001 by Julianna Baggott. Reprinted by permission of the author. "Poetry Despises Your Attempts at Domesticity." Copyright © 2005 by Julianna Baggott. Reprinted by permission of the author.

Barresi, Dorothy. "The Prodigal Daughter," from *The Post-Rapture Diner*, University of Pittsburgh Press. Copyright © 1996 by Dorothy Barresi. Reprinted by permission of University of Pittsburgh Press. "In Waking Words," from *All of the Above*, Beacon Press. Copyright © 1991 by Dorothy Barresi. Reprinted by permission of Beacon Press, Boston.

Beatty, Jan. "Modern Love," from *Boneshaker*, University of Pittsburgh Press. Copyright © 2002 by Jan Beatty. Reprinted by permission of University of Pittsburgh Press. "Pittsburgh Poem," from *Mad River*, University of Pittsburgh Press. Copyright © 1995 by Jan Beatty. Reprinted by permission of University of Pittsburgh Press.

Blaeser, Kimberly. "Dictionary for the New Century" and "What They Did by Lamplight." Copyright © 2005 by Kimberly Blaeser. Reprinted by permission of the author.

Boruch, Marianne. "Sewing," from *A Stick That Breaks and Breaks*, Oberlin College Press. Copyright © 1997 by Oberlin College Press. Reprinted by permission of Oberlin College Press.

Breckenridge, Jill. "Cooking Catalogue," from *How To Be Lucky*, Bluestem Press. Copyright © 1990 by Jill Breckenridge. Reprinted by permission of the author.

Bryner, Jeanne. "Desert Flowers," from *Blind Horse: Poems*, Bottom Dog Press. Copyright © 1999 by Jeanne Bryner. Reprinted by permission of the author. "Part of a Larger Country." Copyright © 2005 by Jeanne Bryner. Reprinted by permission of the author.

Chang, Victoria. "Five-Year Plan," originally published in *Threepenny Review.* Copyright © 2004 by Victoria Chang. Reprinted by permission of the author.

Chin, Marilyn. "The Floral Apron," from *The Phoenix Gone, The Terrace Empty.* Minneapolis: Milkweed Editions, 1994. Copyright © 1994 by Marilyn Chin. Reprinted by permission of Milkweed Editions.

Cisneros, Sandra. "A Man in My Bed Like Cracker Crumbs." From *Loose Woman.* Copyright © 1994 by Sandra Cisneros. Published by Vintage Books, a division of Random House, Inc., and originally in hardcover by Alfred A. Knopf, Inc. Reprinted by permission of Susan Bergholz Literary Services, New York. All rights reserved.

Clifton, Lucille. "quilting," from *Blessing the Boats: New and Selected Poems 1988–2000.* Copyright © 1991, 2000 by Lucille Clifton. Reprinted by permission of BOA Editions, Ltd.

Connolly, Geraldine. "Mother, a Young Wife Learns to Sew," from *Province of Fire,* Iris Press. Copyright © 1998 by Geraldine Connolly. "New House," originally published in *Rattle* #17. Copyright 2002 by Geraldine Connolly. Both poems reprinted by permission of the author.

Crooker, Barbara. "Grating Parmesan," originally published in *Denver Quarterly.* Copyright © 1991 by Barbara Crooker. Reprinted by permission of the author.

Digges, Deborah. "Broom," from *Rough Music,* W. W. Norton and Company, Inc. Copyright © 1997 by Deborah Digges. Reprinted by permission of W. W. Norton and Company, Inc.

Dryansky, Amy. "The Size of a Bed Sheet," from *How I Got Lost So Close to Home,* Alice James Books. Copyright © 1999 by Amy Dryansky. Reprinted by permission of Alice James Books.

Duhamel, Denise. "The Ugly Step Sister," from *Queen for a Day,* University of Pittsburgh Press. Copyright © 2001 by Denise Duhamel. Reprinted by permission of University of Pittsburgh Press.

Erdrich, Heid. "Good Woman," copyright © 2005 by Heid Erdrich. Reprinted by permission of the author. "Sweeping Heaven," from *Fishing for Myth,* New Rivers Press. Copyright © 1997 by Heid Erdrich. Reprinted by permission of the author.

Firer, Susan. "Peonies," from *The Laugh We Make When We Fall,* Backwaters Press, Omaha, NE, 2002. Copyright © 2002 by Susan Firer. Originally appeared in the *Georgia Review.* Reprinted by permission of the author.

Fisher, Diane Gilliam. "After the Miscarriage" and "Sweet Hour," from *One of Everything,* Cleveland State University Poetry Center. Originally appeared in *Spoon River Poetry Review.* Copyright © 2003 by Diane Gilliam Fisher. Both poems reprinted by permission of the author.

Gemin, Pamela. "Upper Peninsula Landscape with Aunts," from *Vendettas, Charms, and Prayers: Poems,* New Rivers Press. Copyright © 1999 by Pamela Gemin. Reprinted by permission of the author.

Harjo, Joy. "Perhaps the World Ends Here," from *The Woman Who Fell From the Sky,* W. W. Norton and Company, Inc. Copyright © 1994 by Joy Harjo. Reprinted by permission of W. W. Norton and Company, Inc.

Iglesias, Holly. "Feeding Frenzy." Copyright © 2005 by Holly Iglesias. "Thursday

Seaton, Maureen. "Furious Cooking," University of Iowa Press. Copyright © 1996 by Maureen Seaton. Reprinted by permission of University of Iowa Press.

Sellers, Heather. "In the Kitchen Dancing to Kitty Wells." Copyright © 2005 by Heather Sellers. Reprinted by permission of the author.

Sergi, Paula. "One Quick Quiz." Copyright © 2005 by Paula Sergi. Reprinted by permission of the author.

Seuss, Diane. "Purpose." Copyright © 2005 by Diane Seuss. Reprinted by permission of the author.

Shearin, Faith. "Entropy" and "The Sinking," from *The Owl Question*, Utah State University Press. Copyright © 2002 by Utah State University Press. Reprinted by permission of Utah State University Press.

Song, Cathy. "Immaculate Lives," from *School Figures*, University of Pittsburgh Press. Copyright © 1995 by Cathy Song. Reprinted by permission of University of Pittsburgh Press. "A Poet in the House" and "The Sky-Blue Dress," from *The Land of Bliss*, University of Pittsburgh Press. Copyright © 2001 by Cathy Song. Reprinted by permission of University of Pittsburgh Press.

Sontag, Kate. "Plum Crazy." Copyright © 2005 by Kate Sontag. Reprinted by permission of the author.

Sutphen, Joyce. "Household Muse," from *Straight Out of View*, Holy Cow! Press. Copyright © 2001 by Joyce Sutphen. Reprinted by permission of Holy Cow! Press.

Sutton, Virginia Chase. "Housekeeping." Copyright © 2005 by Virginia Chase Sutton. Reprinted by permission of the author.

Tibbetts, Elizabeth. "Coming Home," from *In the Well*, Bluestem Press. Originally appeared in *Green Mountains Review*. Copyright © 2003 by Bluestem Press. Reprinted by permission of Bluestem Press.

Townsend, Alison. "Hospital Corners" and "Western Holly Stove." Copyright © 2005 by Alison Townsend. Reprinted by permission of the author.

Townsend, Ann. "Date Nut Bread" and "Day's End," from *Dime Store Erotics*, Silverfish Review Press. Copyright © 1998 by Silverfish Review Press. Reprinted by permission of the author. "The Dinner Guest," from *The Coronary Garden*, Sarabande Books. Copyright © 2005 by Ann Townsend. Reprinted by permission of Sarabande Books.

Trethewey, Natasha. "Domestic Work, 1937" and "Housekeeping," from *Domestic Work*, Graywolf Press. Copyright © 2000 by Natasha Trethewey. Reprinted by permission of Graywolf Press, St. Paul, Minnesota.

Ullman, Leslie. "The History of Women," from *Slow Work through Sand*, University of Iowa Press. Copyright © 1998 by Leslie Ullman. Reprinted by permission of University of Iowa Press.

Vollmer, Judith. "Canning Cellar, Early Sixties," from *The Door Open to the Fire*, Cleveland State University Press. Copyright © 1998 by Judith Vollmer. Reprinted by permission of Cleveland State University Press.

Waring, Belle. "Back to Catfish," from *Refuge*, University of Pittsburgh Press. Copyright © 1990 by Belle Waring. Reprinted by permission of University of Pittsburgh Press.

Index to Titles